SAI BABA

FOR BEGINNERS™

Writers and Readers Publishing, Inc.
P.O. Box 461, Village Station
New York, NY 10014

Writers and Readers Limited
35 Britannia Row
London N1 8QH
Tel: 0171 226 3377
Fax: 0171 359 1454
e-mail: begin@writersandreaders.com

Spanish Edition:
Sai Baba para Principiantes,
published by ERA NACIENTE SLR
Arce 287
Buenos Aires (1426)
Argentina

First Published by Writers and Readers 1998
Text Copyright © 1997 Era Naciente SLR.
Typeset by: Tenth Avenue Editions

A Writers and Readers Documentary Comic Book
Copyright © 1998
ISBN # 0-86316-257-6 Trade
1 2 3 4 5 6 7 8 9 0

Printed in Finland by WSOY

Beginners Documentary Comic Books are published by Writers and Readers Publishing, Inc. Its trademark, consisting of the words "For Beginners, Writers and Readers Documentary Comic Books" and the Writers and Readers logo, is registered in the U. S. Patent and Trademark Office and in other countries.

Writers and Readers

publishing FOR BEGINNERS™ books continuously since 1975

1975:Cuba • 1976: Marx • 1977: Lenin • 1978: Nuclear Power • 1979: Einstein • Freud • 1980: Mao • Trotsky • 1981: Capitalism • 1982: Darwin • Economics • French Revolution • Marx's Kapital • Food • Ecology • 1983: DNA • Ireland • 1984: London • Peace • Medicine • Orwell • Reagan • Nicaragua • Black History • 1985: Marx's Diary • 1986: Zen • Psychiatry • Reich • Socialism • Computers • Brecht • Elvis • 1988: Architecture • Sex • JFK • Virginia Woolf • 1990: Nietzsche • Plato • Malcolm X • Judaism • 1991: WWII • Erotica • African History • 1992: Philosophy • • Rainforests • Miles Davis • Islam • Pan Africanism • 1993: Black Women • Arabs and Israel • 1994: Babies • Foucault • Heidegger • Hemingway • Classical Music • 1995: Jazz • Jewish Holocaust • Health Care • Domestic Violence • Sartre • United Nations • Black Holocaust • Black Panthers • Martial Arts • History of Clowns • 1996: Opera • Biology • Saussure • UNICEF • Kierkegaard • Addiction & Recovery • I Ching • Buddha • Derrida • Chomsky • McLuhan • Jung • 1997: Lacan • Shakespeare • Structuralism • Che • 1998:Fanon • Adler • Marilyn • Postmodernism • Cinema

SAI BABA

BY MARCELO BERENSTEIN
ILLUSTRATED BY MIGUEL ANGEL SCENNA

CONTENTS

"Had I appeared as God, as the Lord himself, they would have put me in a museum and sold tickets to those seeking My Blessing. Had I come as a simple man, they would not have respected my teachings nor followed them for their sake. That's why I came in this human form, with supernatural powers and wisdom".

Why does he say he's God? Why was he anointed with this divine title? What has he come to do in the 20th century? Is he the master or a servant? What does it mean that he has come to celebrate diversity as the only road to unity? Why are his words so familiar to me, if I'm not a Hindu? Could it be that while He is aware of his divinity, we only are so at times? This story does not begin with Him.

...Why was Sai Baba born in **India**? Why is India the place of birth of great religions?

It is hard to understand India with an occidental mind. Within its territory, 900 million people, 14 languages and 544 dialects coexist. Though **Hindi** is the official language, a fourth of the population also speaks English.

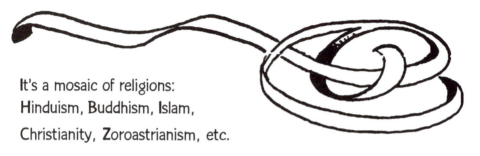

It's a mosaic of religions:
Hinduism, Buddhism, Islam,
Christianity, Zoroastrianism, etc.

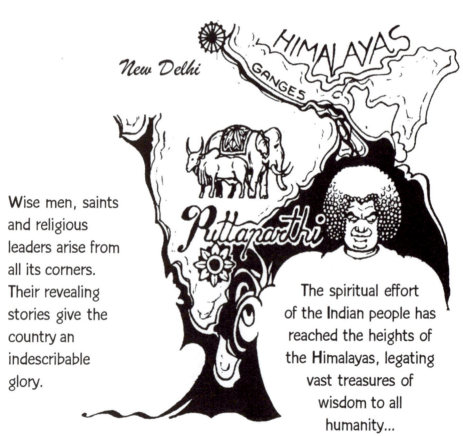

New Delhi

HIMALAYAS

GANGES

Puttaparthi

Wise men, saints and religious leaders arise from all its corners. Their revealing stories give the country an indescribable glory.

The spiritual effort of the Indian people has reached the heights of the Himalayas, legating vast treasures of wisdom to all humanity...

Both Islam and Christianity count thousands of followers all over India.

Mahatma Gandhi, obliged reference among the spiritual leaders, was raised according to strict Hindu traditions.

From a very young age, he showed a peaceful spirit and moral righteousness. English rule distressed him to suffocation, but methodical practice of the sacred precepts produced an inevitable alchemy in his free spirit: it transformed him into a true peace worker. His strategy was to transmute the invader's aggression into nonviolence. With this sole weapon he freed India from the United Kingdom.

The existence of Spiritual Masters (gurus) is fundamental for Hindus: the Spiritual Masters transmit the Holy Scriptures and show God's ways to the common man. They are considered physicians who heal the disease of ignorance, which causes suffering, generating successive births and deaths (Wheel of Reincarnations). An infinite number of Spiritual Masters were born in India.

Sri **Ramakrishna Paramahamsa** is illuminated through the permanent vision of God in all Creation's objects. He transmits his experience through the teachings of the Eternal Religion.

RAMA-KRISHNA (1836 -1886)

1. God exists and can be realized.

2. Realizing God is the purpose of human life.

3. God is one, but His names, forms and aspects can be various, and he too is beyond all description.

4. Every religion is a path to God.

5. The glory of human birth is an expression of the divinity in its masculine and feminine form.

6. Service to man is service to God.

7. The truth of the Lord's incarnation for the suffering humanity.

Some occidental travelers report on the Spiritual Masters. But only at the end of the 19th century do some of the gurus visit the Occident themselves.

· ·

Swami Vivekananda, the disciple of Sri Ramakrishna, arrives in Chicago in 1893. From then on he becomes the spokesman for **Vedanta**: the oldest spiritual tradition in history, a philosophy that shows man his connection with divinity. Some Americans open their eyes toward the inside....

That same year, in a rich Bengali family, a child is born with a clear perception of his divinity. In 1913, **Swami Yogananda** arrives in Chicago and founds the **Self-Realization Fellowship**. He writes simply and deeply on **Yoga**. Americans consider it a physic-spiritual gym.

· ·

"*Do not go after gurus who suffer from imperfect vision or domestic problems. Ask nothing from individuals who are beggars themselves. Avoid all vanity and competence among you. Let each one go at his pace, but may the road and the direction lead to God.*"

The jungle is the world. The lion is the fear that obliges us to engage in worldly activities (samsara). The bear is the anxiety that makes us cling to actions and attachments. The roots, one in each hand, represent hope and discouragement. The rats represent day and night, which end with our lifetime. Hanging, we fight to reach a bit of joy, tasting the drops of selfishness and possessions. When we find that the honey is out of our reach, we despair in search of a guide. The master appears either from our own interior or as a real living being when we give up the illusory ego.

Along with the guru's presence, there are avatars. Avatar means Divine Incarnation in human form: God on Earth. Their conception and birth have special characteristics that distinguish them. Though they walk and talk like us, the avatars are free from the ties other humans have: they have no attachments. In their bodies they condense truth, love, righteousness, peace and nonviolence. They are beyond the principle of cause and effect (karma). They appear when humanity needs to recuperate its human values. Buddha was an avatar.

*E*arthly goods impede the knowledge of true richness. Castes get their status in virtue of the culture and not from acquired merits. Desires do nothing but create frustration once what is longed for has been reached. I give up everything.

I will descend under the southern snows of the Himalayas, where a just king lives.
That night Maya dreams of a star that discharges a flash of light that penetrates her and installs in her womb.

Rama (He who pleases) continues to be venerated by millions of Hindus. To them Rama is the very essence of the **Veda**, their most sacred scriptures. His life is one revelation of the divine purpose after another. He reestablishes virtue, or the Dharma (the internal principle of religion), destroyed by King Ravana's vandalism.

His fame spread beyone his native Ayodhya.

Wherever he goes, he is recognized as the Avatar. Each one of his acts represents a teaching.

According to tradition,the union of Rama with Sita transcends the usual significance of marriage. She personifies love, peace and, above all, joy. Sita imparted to Rama the divinity's feminine aspect.

What is an avatar?
When is he born? And what for?

When humanity finds itself in the midst of a spiritual crisis, beings appear that, according to Indian tradition, are known as avatars or complete incarnations of the Divinity. This means that they can manifest:

- **Omnipotence** (total control over energy and matter).
- **Omnipresence** (be in several places at the same time).
- **Omniscience** (know absolutely everything, have absolute conscience).

Even though not everybody gets to known them, their presence on Earth is to help the spiritual growth of all men, without distinction. Indian culture describes ten avatars. Nine have already shown up. Sathya Sai Baba recognizes himself as the tenth—avatar Kalki— who will take humanity to the Golden Age. In numerous messages he announces the advent of a time of peace, love and happiness.

The flute is man. God
plays his melody through
us.

Krishna incarnated God to restore spiritual consciousness. He
devised the **Mahabharata,** an epic poem venerated by the Hindus.
In this battle, Krishna has a beloved disciple, **Arjuna**. Through him,
Krishna speaks to the world.

The battle between Kauravas
and Pandavas represents the
fight between light and
darkness. Arjuna, a Pandava,
represents goodness,
service.

The Kauravas represent
attachments, avarice, envy,
ire, hatred, jealousy and lust.

The carriage symbolizes the
mind. The horses, the five
senses. When we give up
the reins of the mind to
God, we keep the senses
from running away.

Yet if this is too difficult, give up being attached to the results of your acts and offer them to God. The offering of your acts shouldn't be a mere verbal exercise. Watch your ways through the word, your work and your thought. Those devoted to the Lord need to be free from hate and full of Love. They must also express their love as a service to fellow beings. Just planting the seed is not enough. The field must be watered and fertilized. The extirpation of hate and the sowing of Love constitute only the first stage. The next step is to eliminate the feeling of "what's mine, is mine and what's yours, is yours".

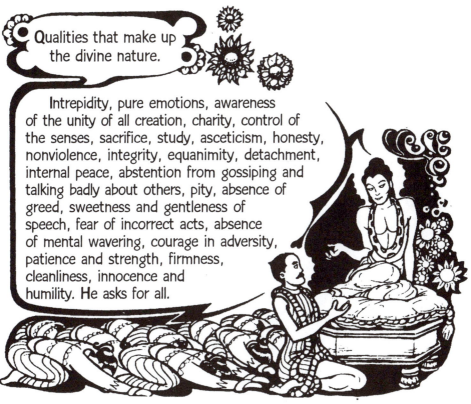

Qualities that make up the divine nature.

Intrepidity, pure emotions, awareness of the unity of all creation, charity, control of the senses, sacrifice, study, asceticism, honesty, nonviolence, integrity, equanimity, detachment, internal peace, abstention from gossiping and talking badly about others, pity, absence of greed, sweetness and gentleness of speech, fear of incorrect acts, absence of mental wavering, courage in adversity, patience and strength, firmness, cleanliness, innocence and humility. He asks for all.

As Rama's mission was to restore Dharma, Krishna's mission was to crown Love as the only path to self-realization. His Love perforated the hardest of hearts, melting them. Even today he is considered the Father of fathers, the Mother of all mothers.

The only way to celebrate the birth of Christ is to lead a life of service based on Love.

I am the son of God. Through **Me** you will reach the Father.

Jesus of Nazareth framed a special moment in human history. There was a history before and after His arrival. He exposed the hypocrisy. He was a model of human perfection. He defeated suffering. He originated the major revolution in history: the Revolution of Love.

Jesus had an unusual conception. Gabriel the archangel, sent by God, visited Mary, a virgin married to Joseph.

You have found grace in the eyes of God. You shall conceive in your womb and give birth to a son whom you will call Jesus.

How will this be? I know no male.

The Holy Spirit will descend upon you and the power of the Almighty will cover you with His shade. For this the saint to be born will be called the son of God.

In spite of lacking a Christian tradition, the Asian continent was strongly influenced by Jesus. India was the most open to receiving his message and considering him an avatar. His image was diffused on a popular level and numerous Hindu thinkers dedicated articles, conferences and books to him.

"Through the manifestation of his love, Christ made it easier for us to have faith in love, and by it live a truer life in the world that He calls the Kingdom of God."

••• Rabindranath Tagore •••

Today, millions of people all over the world consider Sathya Sai Baba to be the avatar of this age. His life expresses the essence of all religions. His message updates the word of the other avatars. His work is a practical manifestation of God's action.

There is only one religion, that of Love.

There is only one race, the human.

There is only one language, the heart's.

There is only one God, and omnipresent.

Dividing men because of their religion is a crime against humanity. Whatever each one's religion is, cultivate respect for the other religions. He who does not have such an attitude of tolerance and respect towards other religions is not a true follower of one's own.

A legend relates how the south of India started its transformation from a cow-town to an ant town.

A cobra used to like to suck his milk straight from the cow's teats. It seems the cow liked it too: every morning she would walk to the cobra's nest and go back with no milk. One day, her shepherd followed her. Discovering the action, he killed the cobra with a stone. The cobra cursed the town: It shall turn sterile.

*Y*ear after year, the cattle were reduced, and so were the men who made their living from them. The only thing that grew were the ants.

*P*uttaparthi, as the village came to be called, means "town of anthills".

Sathya Sai Baba was born and raised in this small village. His presence, life, miracles, and especially. His works constitute an actual divine magnet that turned Puttaparthi into a multitudinous pilgrimage hub. Millions of people, from all corners of the planet, from all races and religions, come to experience the God that incarnates in Him.

The miracle of Sai Baba's conception

When the Cosmic Conscience decides to take on a human role and incarnate as an avatar, he chooses the time and place to be born. He also selects his parents. Sai Baba chose Pedda and Easwarama, a very respected couple from Puttaparthi. Both felt a strong devotion to God. By chance or design, **Easwarama** means "mother of God".

My mother-in-law had a dream with God. After waking she warned me not to fear. If something should happen, it would be the Lord's will.

That morning, I went to the well and when I was taking the water out, a great ball of light came rolling towards me. In this way I became pregnant.

Years later, Sai Baba would say:
"More than a pregnancy, it was an admission".

During the gestation, sweet melodies would awake the father by night. The music sprang spontaneously from the chord and wind instruments at home. Angels? Spirits? Demons? Magic? Foregone musicians? The man decides to ask an astrologer.

Is the music sweet and quiet?

It's always very nice.

Are there any pregnant women in the house?

Yes, my wife Easwarama.

The gods play the music to please the child that lies within your wife's womb.

The chosen time

November 23, 1926

The Grandmother puts the baby on a kind of small mattress with a thick blanket in a corner of the room.

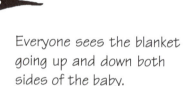

Everyone sees the blanket going up and down both sides of the baby.

A rolled-up cobra appears on the mattress. For the Hindus, the cobra is a symbol of divinity. The god Shiva has one coiled around the neck. They say the god Vishnu rested on the rings of a snake.

The little one is baptized **Sathyanarayana**.

His friends follow him as a religious leader. Soon he becomes a spiritual teacher for the whole village. He loves animals. He is a strict vegetarian.

He begs his companions not to take part in the ox cart races; even less in cock fights. Sathya does not listen to his elders' advice when they warn him about the animals' unpredictable and aggressive character. His love for all without distinction begins to grow.

Why is that child so much like the others and yet so different? What magnet does he have to attract children, men, beggars, the erudite...?

His behavior is exemplary. He venerates his parents as he venerates God himself. He never fights with anyone. Aggression simply doesn't exist in Sathya. His good conduct starts to intrigue his family.

Family poverty does not stop him from living in order to give. In spite of his parents' annoyance, he usually brings beggars and the crippled home for meals. Often, he goes without food to give his portion to those who are most in need. He never desires anything. He satisfies himself with little. He is extremely intelligent. His arguments are always invincible. His thinking is faster than any adult's. His feelings are profound and lasting. He speaks gently.

Sathya walks two and a half miles every day to get to school. The village people have already heard of him, receiving him with all honors.

Some of his classmates are jealous of the way Sathya is treated. When they push or pound him, Sathya never tells on anyone.

Sathya makes different things materialize in order to give them to his classmates. Fruits, marbles, candy, pencils...

Since Sathya is the best student in the class, the teacher names him headmaster and authorizes him to punish the others when they do something wrong.

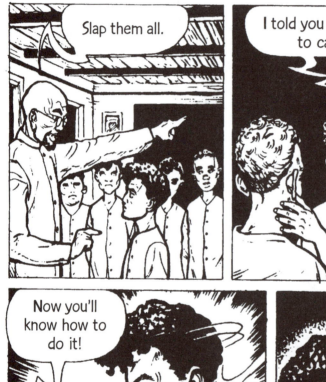

"The man is a pilgrim who has already come a long way from birth to birth. The road he has walked determines what remains to pass".

Another teacher, Kondapa, learns who Sathya is the hard way. Dictating notes one day, he notes the student does not obey him.

The teacher is only able to move away from the chair when Sathya wants. Ever after, Kondapa and the rest of the teachers start to venerate Sathya too. Years later, Sai Baba remarks that thanks to that incident many people began to realize he was a Divine Child.

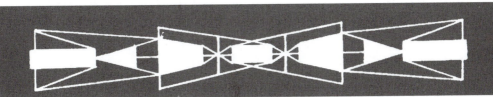

At nine, Sathya is a complete artist. He sings and dances. He composes songs and poems. Obviously, his art holds a social mission. One day he sets upon the richest man in town, who proudly displays his Hitler style mustache. The song composed by Sathya shows the dark side of the man and, to top it off, he makes the mustache disappear from his face. Other village notables feel obliged to change their pernicious habits. Illiteracy, prostitution, agricultural debts and drinking are the issues the prodigious young man combats.

Even today people remember what happened when a popular dance and drama company touring the region reached Puttaparthi.

Oh, he picked up a needle with his eyelids...

One day, a cart enters the village at full speed. The driver looks for the prodigious child who makes ashes from nothing. Finding Sathya, he tells him he wants those ashes to "heal" the engine of his jeep that has broken down on the road. "My master is furious", he says.

Warning a white man, an Englishman with a rifle in his hand! Stopping his jeep and refusing to give him what he asked for! And also, scolding him...Sathya's parents start fearing for their son's mental health.

His hardest trials

Sathya's growing fame provokes adoration and hate in the settlers. He is both venerated and persecuted to the same degree. His parents too are as respected as they are denigrated. His mother vascillates between seeing her son's divinity and believing he is a victim of sorcery. His father, backed by Sathya's older brother, seems to have no doubt.

Sathya is possessed by a nasty spirit from the inferior worlds!

Sathya's strange actions bewilder his father. Day by day, his compassion dwindles. His mind, influenced by popular belief, attributes all deviation from the norm to the schemes of a rival, to witch rites or the devil's design. Father and brother put Sathya through painful physical punishment to try and "straighten out" the rebel.

Since the battering therapy has no effect, the family sends Sathya to live with another brother, who has been named schoolmaster in another village sixty two miles from Puttaparthi.

Living at his brother's house is not pleasant for Sathya. He has to walk half a mile six times a day to get water.

· ·

They can't abuse your kindness. Why must they depend on you for water?

I feel it as a duty. How much longer will those children survive if they drink polluted water? It's a pleasure to bring them the water of life. I've come to render this service.

Once, Sathya is absent for a week to participate in a boy scouts camp, and nobody bothers to go for water. Once back, his brother's family reprehends him severely, hitting him on his hands with a rod.

· ·

Why are your hands bandaged?

...

With his silence, Sathya shows respect for his elders.

To Sathya, friendship is something sacred. A friend constitutes a gift from God. The other is "another I", someone who experiences with equal intensity our own joy and sadness. Sathya would never have chosen a friend for money, power, social position.

At twelve, his close friends are Ramesh and Sudhir. Being excellent students, the three have the chance to participate in scout camp. They have to wear uniforms. Sathya can't afford to buy one. Ramesh, a rich merchant's son, offers him a new one, from the heart. Sathya returns it to him with a note.

If you want our friendship to last, you shouldn't take part in this material give-and-take game. When a person in need accepts something from a rich man, anxiety stays on the watch in his mind for a way of returning the favor, while pride contaminates the giver's mind, on account of his act of "charity"...

True friendship should be from heart to heart. If we build friendship on the basis of give and take, the receiver feels small and the giver proud. Such a friendship will not last. So I will not take the clothes that you have put here. I'm returning them to you.

Sathya

The Annunciation

It's 7 P.M. on Thursday the 7th of March, 1940. Sathya is washing his hands when, apparently, he is bit by a scorpion. The next day, at the same time, he passes out. Ever after, his personality suffers serious transmutations. The mystery of his mysterious ways grows deeper. The youth develops an unusual behavior pattern on the physical, mental and spiritual levels.

The transcendental self is an ocean without bottom or coasts. Swim calmly with joy in this deep ocean, only then will you reach peace.

Knowing what has happened, his parents travel to join Sathya immediately. On the way, Easwarama only asks God for her son to be normal. Meanwhile, Sathya recovers consciousness, but refuses to eat or drink. Nothing occurring around him affects him at all. He seems to be talking to invisible beings out in the universe. Astrologers, homeopaths, priests, fortune tellers, natural healers, Ayurvedic doctors, all fail in the intent to bring him back to normal. Downcast by pain, his parents decide to take him back to Puttaparthi with them.

Going home changes nothing. Sathya remains estranged from all that goes on around him. In a sacred text, his grandfather discovers that avatar Rama went through a similar listlessness at the same age.

"His body grew thin, his mind fluttering from one idea to the other, he would remain seated, in silence, as if he were painted on the wall.

We don't know what to do with him.

The father is truth, mother is love, adore parents as God himself.

Is Sathya ill? Is he a madman or a saint? A genius or a joker? Is it possible that this boy of abnormal and rebellious behavior could really be a Divine Being? Just in case, his sisters write down all he says.

Afraid of their mother, his sisters destroy everything they write. To Sathya nothing seems to matter. Anguish corrodes the family roots. The atmosphere at home grows increasingly tense. Everybody MIND fluctuates between faith and despair.

He's the guru of gurus!!

LEAVE HIM ALONE!!

He's possessed by a spirit.

When they understand they're not a body, attachments and deceits will vanish.

They decide to take him to an exorcist in a nearby village. This medicine man boasts of having defeated all kinds of spirits. The power of his mantras, they say, is capable of driving away the most Mephis-tophelian ones. The treat-ment he gives Sathya deserves to be counted in the Guinness book of terror.

Sathya does not react to the pain. His face does not show the least trace of fear. His passive attitude infuriates the exorcist even more, so he decides to give him some "intensive medicine" (sic). He shaves his head. Then he makes a deep cut in the shape of a cross on the scalp. Not content with this, he squeezes lemon juice over the wounds, then pours frozen water over Sathya. Later, he uses a corrosive paste that burns the skin. Sathya's eyes become inflamed, his face swollen. But only Holy Scriptures verses come out of his mouth.

You can take your child but the spirit within him belongs to me.

Have God's name on your tongues and God's form in front of your minds' eye. This is the most elevated spiritual practice.

Sathya's fame increases along with his family's suffering. More and more people crowd around Sathya. The devoted, the desperate, the curious and the cynical surround him constantly, wherever he may be, wherever he should go. Desperate, his father and mother send for Krishnamachari, a prestigious lawyer from a nearby village. The lawyer accepts, without a thought: he wants to meet the child personally. Many times he has heard of his paranormal powers. After seeing him, the lawyer gives his verdict.

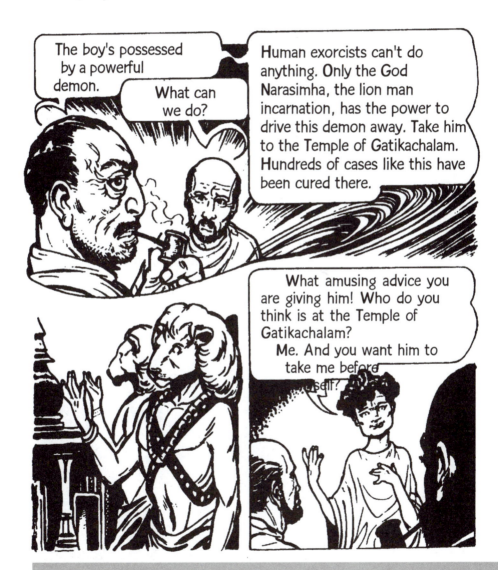

The boy's possessed by a powerful demon.

What can we do?

Human exorcists can't do anything. Only the God Narasimha, the lion man incarnation, has the power to drive this demon away. Take him to the Temple of Gatikachalam. Hundreds of cases like this have been cured there.

What amusing advice you are giving him! Who do you think is at the Temple of Gatikachalam? Me. And you want him to take me before myself?

The boy's attitude confuses his family even more.
At thirteen, Sathya decides to end the illusion created around him.
He goes up on his grandfather's roof. A crowd watches him in
amazement. Under a simple circular motion of his right hand, candy
and flowers start to appear from the air. He materializes the right
amount so that everyone gets his present.

Sai Baba??? The name is practically unknown in the area until someone finds out that it belonged to a Man-God who lived in a northern India town called Shirdi.

. . . .

It's better for him to be delirious thinking of himself as an unknown saint than to go about yelling he is the incarnation of God himself.

It won't be long before Sathya gives another proof of his identity. A friend of the family, who lives in a village nearby, informed about the boy's audacious revelation, wants to unmask him. Be that as it may.

I'm sure you're a liar. Anyway I'll give you the opportunity to prove I'm wrong. If you are the same Sai Baba my local Register Office's manager venerates, give us a sign. Now!

You may think miracles attract people and generate attachments towards me. This is not so. They are spontaneous proofs of My Divinity.

After that day, Sathya's character begins to improve. He does not show himself as unfriendly. He seems nicer. He happily responds to family requests. But this does not mean he gives up his belief of feeling himself to be an incarnated divinity. On the contrary, the fantastic events multiply and the village people require his advice.

His brother takes him to his house again, and little by little Sathya's life goes back to how it was before, with blows, abuse and humiliations.

The revelation

October, 1940. Civil servants from a city nearby invite Sathya for a
visit. His brother takes him, secretly hoping that a change of air will
improve his mental health. They are shown the ruins of Hampi, capital
of a famous empire. Within the ruins, they visit the temple of
Virupakshja. The group goes about admiring the architecture and
sculptures. Reaching the Sancta Satorum, the priest guiding them
goes ahead to light the camphor flame to show them the deity.

Sai Baba's smiling face on the stone sculpture leaves them
dumbfounded. Some are left perplexed in the presence of what they
see, others run away: That **is** Sathya!

Guess who the runners find at the ruins' door? Yes, Sathya himself is there. He is contemplating the sky in solitude. How can he be in two places at the same time?

By means of the divine interior force, man can do anything, even become God.

For the authorities of Hospet there is no doubt: Sathya is a divine presence. When he leaves, they see him off with the honors and religious pomp a Child-God deserves.

Sathya goes back to his brother's house and returns to school. But his behavior gets weirder all the time. One October morning of 1940, he goes to school, says hello to his classmates. He goes with them to say the daily prayers, but once they are over...

From now on, I don't belong to you anymore! I belong to everyone! I am Sathya Sai Baba! My mission has begun!

Surrender your mind at the feet of the guru. He will get you through life's turbulence.

After the announcement, he goes to a nearby rock. First he pronounces a sermon, then he sings his first bajhan.

The word is out all over the region. Monday's fair is the area's sensationalist news agency. All that is heard there is reproduced and multiplied in the neighboring towns. News about Sathya's behavior does not take long to be diffused. But it comes out as a rumor, and deformed. "He's run to Shirdi", "He's gone yogi", "He went clandestine", "His car went up and vanished in the sky", "He disintegrated to become jasmine petals"...

Each Puttaparthi inhabitant has his own version. The grapevine tangle reaches Sathya's parents' house. They decide to travel to Uravonkonda in search of the truth. At the bus station, someone recognizes them and hands them a letter from their older son.

Sathya is alive, well and still finds himself in Uravakonda. He's gone, but is back home, though he lives as a stranger. It appears that in the school he announced there was nothing he should learn there. He threw the books far from the house and went to sit on a rock in front of the tax inspector's house. This man pays cult to him every Thursday. Your son has assumed the position of the Father of the World: he has a great deal of devotees who plead to see him and receive his blessing.

SHESHAMA.

At Sheshama's house, a crowd struggles to get in and catch a glimpse of the Child-God.

With great effort, his parents manage to get in and try to speak with Sathya. The youth does not seem to be aware of their presence until his brother asks him:

Who are they?

They are Maya.*

The devastating answer chills those who observe the scene. Torn by the pain, Easwarama faints and falls. His father realizes that all the talk about his son's divinity is true.

In the New Testament, Matthew describes an anecdote of striking resemblance: "While Jesus was talking to the people, his mother and brothers were outside, wanting to talk to Him. Someone approached him and said: 'Your mother and Your brothers are outside and want to have a word with you'. He answered them: 'Who is My mother and who My brothers? The one doing My Father's will who is in heaven, that one is My brother, My sister, My mother".

The love I feel for you is that of a thousand mothers.

*Maya: cosmic illusion, that which is apparent.

46

I'm no longer your Sathya. I'm Sai Baba's reincarnation, I will leave the world at 96 and come back as Prema Sai Baba.

Sai Baba of Shirdi's reincarnation? Come back as Prema Sai Baba? Does he mean he is not one but three? If it's true that he is God, is the world so bad off that he has to come three times in a row? Who was this mysterious Sai Baba of Shirdi?

Once there was a humble boatman, devoted to Master Shiva. His wife, prayed to Parvathi, Shiva's feminine aspect, every day. Both were kind and helpful, but they could not have children. Until the unexpected happened. One stormy night, while the man was working, an old man called at the house door. The woman answered. The old man asked for some clothes and something to eat. She gave him some food and let him sleep on the doorway. A while later, the old man knocked on the door again. This time he begged to be given massages on his leg. Surprised by the request, the woman went to the women next door. They refused, saying they were busy. Confused, the woman asked Parvathi for help. Then she heard a sudden noise behind the door. When she opened it, she met a woman who offered to massage the old man. She took her to him and shut the door. Again, a loud noise startled her. She ran to open. A brilliant light blinded her. What she saw and heard made her kneel down out of devotion.

And so it was.

When the first two sons had finished their adolescence, the woman got pregnant for the third time. In that time, her husband was possessed by an intense desire to realize God. He began to lose interest in the family and working matters. Soon, the longing became obsession. He decided to retire to the woods in search of illumination. His wife, moved by love and respect for traditions, decided to go with her husband. The children stayed with their grandmother. The couple entered deep into the forest. A few days later, the woman had labor pains. She asked her husband to wait for her, but he did not hear her and went on. Agitated, she stopped under a great banana tree, closed her eyes, pushed hard and gave birth. With the big leaves of the tree she made a cradle for the baby. She gave him a kiss and left him to go after her husband.

The abandoned creature is the very same Shiva! There is no way he could die of cold or hunger a few hours after birth: that's not worthy of a divinity.
Yet, God gives human life stories the most surprising endings. Another married couple, Muslim, was walking through the forest. Suddenly, the woman needed to go to the bathroom. She had no alternative but to go behind a tree. And—oh, coincidence!—she chose the same one where the child had been left. The couple, who had no children either, decided the baby was a gift from Allah and adopted him. They named him Babu.

Babu is not a common and ordinary boy. His behavior worries his family too. At the mosque, he arranges and adores an oval-shaped stone, which the Hindus call lingam and venerate strongly. This irritates the Muslims. When Babu goes to the Hindu temples he recites the Koran, inciting the assistants' anger.

One day, while playing marbles with the son of a high official, he wins them all. The boy, infuriated, goes to his family's altar, takes the lingam and bets it. Babu wins again. The boy tells his mother what has happened. When she goes to claim it from him, Babu puts it in his mouth and swallows it. The woman demands that he give it back. What she sees changes her life forever: looking inside Babu's mouth, she has a cosmic vision—the same one Yashoda had in Krishna's mouth, many centuries earlier.

When Babu's adoptive father dies, his wife gives Babu up to an ashram for orphans. The boy is received with all honors. The people don't understand why a Muslim child is admitted to a Hindu ashram. Very few know that the night before, the guru had dreamt of Shiva, who told him he would present himself in the form of a Muslim child. During his stop at the ashram, the guru devoted himself to give the child the highest spiritual precepts. Babu lived there until the death of his master.

After leaving the ashram, the young fakir wanders through different cities of the region. Finally, in 1857, he settles down in an abandoned mosque of Shirdi. His presence arouses all kinds of remarks: Who is this man of such enigmatic looks? What drives him to dress combining the Hindu and Muslim traditions? Shortly after arriving, a neighbor that had met him at the ashram recognizes him and calls him Sai Baba. •

One morning of 1886, Sai Baba tells a disciple he will meditate for three days in a row. "I want to talk to Allah", he says, lying down. As soon as he closes his eyes he enters into meditation. Shortly after, he stops breathing. He is "dead". It does not take long for the news to spread. The house gets packed with village people who intone devotional songs, expecting a miracle. On the fourth day, Sai Baba returns to his body!

Ever since, he has dedicated his life to teaching the highest spiritual precepts. His action inspires Hindus and Muslims to leave differences aside. His message mellows the area's tense atmosphere. Sai Baba turns Shirdi into a center of constant pilgrimage. People come from all over India. Not only Hindus and Muslims, but also Buddhists, Jainists, Zoroastrians, Sheiks...Nobody coming from Shirdi is let down or angry.

I give you what you want so that you follow me and accept what I want to give you.

October 15, 1918.

Look for me in Puttaparthi, eight years from now.

Allah is putting out the lamp that he himself has lit.

Throughout history, the planet has always had avatars, gurus and saints. Some of them accomplished their missions taking their messages here and there, wandering about like Sai Baba of Sirdhi. Others, instead, did their job in a determined place. Obviously, Sai Baba's presence was an attraction that captivated a great deal of people. Many other leaders had faithful acolytes and beloved disciples. Naturally, around these Beings small communities arose, which grew as the number of followers increased.

These settlements are known as ashrams. In these communities, residents and visitors carry out spiritual and ascetic practices. They are true schools for inner growth and transformation. The Orient, and especially India, features the largest number of ashrams. These may be millenary and modern, feed and free, with free or selective entrance.

Master	Ashram	Place
Sri Ramana Maharshi	Aruna Achala Ramana	Tiruvanamalai
Sri Ramakrishna Paramahamsa	Ramkrishna Belur Math	Bwer (West Bengala)
Swami Sivananda	Society of the Divine Life	Rishikesh
Swami Vivekananda	Vivekananda Ashram	Trivandrum
Sri Aurobindo	Auroville	Pondicherry
Sathya Sai Baba	Prashanti Nilayam*	Puttaparthi

*Prashanti Nilayam means "House of the Supreme Peace"

Boy Sathya becomes Bhagavan Sri Sathya Sai Baba. Back in Puttaparthi he refuses to live with his family. He feels that such an over-possessive and selfish love oppresses him. He stops belonging to his family and surrenders to the one he feels as true: humanity. He belongs to all, not a few. He establishes himself in a rich family's home, whose members recognize his divinity. He stays there until 1944, when he decides to live alone.

. . . .

The news that Sathya has come home transforms the rural village into a pilgrimage hub for hundreds of people from neighboring towns. Most of them come to benefit from his healing powers rather than to seek spiritual realization. The sick, possessed, hopeless come with their pain. Sai Baba finds time to attend to each one of them.

These notes, written by a devout person who visited Sai Baba in 1942, show the hardships they had to go through to get to Puttaparthi.

My Mission has begun

"These are my words for you, My devotees. Each one of you has an essential role to accomplish during this life. Only those whom I have called can serve me.

My Mission has reached the point in which each one of you has a job to do. This planet has a purpose in the great galaxy it belongs to. This purpose unfolds before our eyes right now. I call you so that you'll irradiate Devotion within yourselves, so its invisible power will cover all those approaching you. To do your part successfully, always keep yourselves centered in Me. Allow yourselves to share the purity of heart inside you with all human beings and all living creatures, and do not obtain fruits from your work.

This part of My Mission is to be carried out in absolute silence. You are My instruments from where My Love will be poured.

Always be conscious that the moment you let your ego overcome you, My work is detained. When you have triumphed over your negativity, again you will become My well. My love will multiply all around the world. I have prepared you by many incarnations. I have attracted you to Me. I have made big advances in My Mission in your past incarnations. My work does not stop, and so your task will never end either. Know that I am inside and outside of you. You are I and I am You. There is no difference. My darshan will be poured from Me to and by You. Perhaps you are not aware of this constant action. Free yourselves from trivial things forever. Always be pure in heart and soul, and humanity will benefit from the special qualities you possess during your entire life. Other people will also join Me in this Mission when I call them. The time is near when all humanity will live in harmony. This will happen a lot sooner than you imagine. Until that time comes, be prepared for anything you can do to reveal the true meaning of existence to a living being. Nobody can even imagine it. It is beyond all understanding. I can tell you its beauty is so magnificent, that no one could even dream it. While you are doing your work in silence, I will hold you against My heart.

From now on your souls will rise and your eyes will show My Presence. I communicate this to My devout from the Summit of the Mountain of the Lord, where all Universes are ONE.

Be near My work. Your breath will carry the flowers' perfume to heaven.

Your example will be that of the Angels.

Your joy will be my happiness".

His first ashram

The attention Sai Baba pays to his devotees rewards the journey's hardships. His first community is a humble temple, smaller than 43 square feet. On one side there is a gallery for men, on the other, another for women.

> For each step you take towards me, I will take a hundred to you.

As the number of visitors increases, the temple gets bigger. Soon it has a main praying room for about 30 thirty people. A little later a small room is built for Sai at a terrain's edge. At night, the devotees sleep outdoors, men and women always separately.

As the number of visitors increases more and more, Sai Baba builds another, much bigger, ashram four blocks away. He personally supervises the work. On the day of his twenty-fifth birthday, he inaugurates Prashanti Nilayam—The House of the Eternal Peace. A group of devotees carries Him on a decorated palanquin. The four blocks separating the ashrams are overwhelmed with men and women from all walks of life. Sai Baba casts handfuls of jasmines and roses over the crowd. While falling, the petals turn to silver memorial coins. November 23 of 1950 is taken as the date of birth of a new spirituality.

Now you can get there by bus or train. Puttaparthi is a hundred miles from Bangalore, along a paved road. Fourteen miles before the ashram, a pink and light blue arch stands erect, on whose top two angels hold the emblem of Sai Baba's organization: the Sarva Dharma, an open flower showing each face of its petals as a symbol of the union of all religions.

A few miles on, after crossing a second arch, there is an airport and, close by, a modern hospital, the Sathya Sai Hospital of Super Medical Specialties. Along the way are the university, the schools, the stadium and the planetarium. There is also a dairy (*Gokulam*) and the house of Sai Gita (Sai Baba's little elephant), another arch and the beginning of Puttaparthi's urban area. Two hundred seventy three yards away is Sai Baba's ashram, called Prashanti Nilayam, House of the Supreme Peace.

In the last ten years, Sai Baba's ashram has become a real city. On less crowded days, five to six thousand people live there. For Sai Baba's sixty fifth birthday, there were a million and a half. All of them ate and were housed there. But what most amazes any visitor is not the agglomeration but the harmony in which Arab and Jewish, Japanese and American, Serb and Croatian, black and white devotees live together...

The true sign of humanity in man is the harmony between mind, word and action. When these three aspects are not unified, human beings turn demoniac.

The true sign of humanity in man is the harmony between mind, word and action. When these three aspects are not unified, human beings turn demoniac.

One hundred and eighty yards beyond the first entrance is the principal arcade, by which Sai Baba goes in and out and which leads to the place where he walks among his visitors, offering his presence (known as darshan). Inside the ashram there is a main street, where the administrative offices are. There is also a bookstore, where you can get books by or about Sai Baba in many languages.

Entering the ashram is going deep into an adventure of new emotions, sensations and livings. The energetic difference between the ashram and the outside is perceived at once. The ashram's ambiance exudes an elevating atmosphere that is contagious. It is impossible not to differentiate between a life that is dedicated to the mundane and one that is dedicated to the spiritual.

Inside the ashram there are a number of three-story buildings, and several round buildings for the devotees to stay in. The rooms are simple spaces where four or five people sleep. They have no beds. People sleep on mats arranged on the floor. The original buildings didn't have any showers—only a faucet at medium height and a plastic jar to pour water from. Obviously there is no hot water, or a kitchen either. Millions of people pass through Prashanti Nilayam every year. When the buildings are full, visitors stay in the sheds. Each person sets up his own space with a mosquito net fastened to the parabolic ceiling. The look of these sheds resembles a field hospital.

Man is the reflection of God,
the individual soul is the reflection
of the universal soul.

The temple's ornaments, or *Mandir*, painted in light blue, pink and yellow, represent different aspects of the multiple Hindu mythology. In its covered gallery (the veranda) sit the students and teachers, the school's and hospital's board members, and Sai Baba's special guests. At the end of the veranda is a small chamber—the room where Sai Baba receives his devotees in private interviews.

Thousands of people wait for the sacred instant when Sai Baba crosses the Mandir.

A day at the ashram

At Prashanti Nilayam, the days repeat themselves in identical fashion, one after another. Activities start before dawn at the temple. At 4 A.M., the ones able to get up repeat the Om twenty one times. This activity is called *Omkar*. The number of visitors has increased so much that the temple gets packed, and many people repeat them from the outside. The entire ashram wakes up with the Om.

Om is the primary sound that impregnates all the Universe. It is what God first created and, by it, realized creation.

As soon as the Omkar finishes, a hymn is sung to wake God: the *Suprabhatam*. Its melody and meaning are incredibly sweet.

They sing as if the angels and archangels were massaging their vocal chords...

One of the steps in man's pilgrimage to God, through dedication and surrender, is singing the Lord's actions in praise of his magnificence and multiple deeds.

Wake up, Oh Sathya! The works of the divinity you have assumed are to be done... Wake up so the world achieves happiness. We pray for an auspicious day, blessed by your vigil.
Moved by the wish of receiving your blessing we are delighted to recite the Vedas' mantras.

They say the one who recites these hymns daily reaches the Supreme Dwelling.

Singing procession

Once the hymn is over, people walk to Ganesha's altar (in front of one of the ashram's doors) and form three lines. In the first are the Brahmins (Hindu priests), in the next, the women, and in the third, the men. They cover the ashram singing Veda hymns and devotional songs so those still sleeping wake up with God's names in their hearts.

Vision of the Divine Being

The following activity is the most awaited moment of the day: Sai Baba walking among his devotees and visitors. It is called *darshan*, vision of the Divine Being. For sensitive souls it's the supreme experience.

Darshan

When Sai Baba appears, it is as if time stopped. It creates such a strong reverential atmosphere that it involves everyone. Many cry. All, without exception, spontaneously put their hands together. Some lose their breath. They can't believe what is happening to them: their own eyes are beholding the presence of the Divinity. Others kneel down or bend forward, surrendering to him. Every day of the year, every year, Sai Baba covers the same route.

His walk is very gentle (it is as if he were not grounding the soles of his feet). He goes barefoot. Always with the orange colored tunic, impeccably pressed. He looks at some, takes letters, talks; he seems to ignore others. Everyone departs with a message.

Now and then he stops, listening to what somebody says to him. He always answers with a useful teaching for everyone listening.

Love is the essential thing.
In the mind it is truth,
in the feeling it is peace, in the knowledge
it is nonviolence and respect,
and in the action it is morality and righteous life.

Sai Baba knows the contents of the letters before opening them. His answers reach every corner of the planet in many different ways. He is omnipresent.

At the end of his walk he receives a group of visitors he has chosen along the way. In the private interview, he answers personal questions and gives spiritual teachings.

Every day some have the grace of seeing him materialize ashes that for the believers have the property to heal. They're known as *vibhuti*. Those receiving these little lumps in their hands say they still preserve a certain warmth. Though they might seem insignificant, Sai Baba considers vibhuti as his most important manifestation.

As Jesus would say:
"From dust we come and to dust we shall return".

For most visitors, after the darshan the day continues with some spiritual practice.

The tree of meditation is an enormous banana tree, where Sai Baba used to sit to meditate when he was a child. Located inside the same ashram, it can be reached coming up the road that leads to the Museum of the Religions.

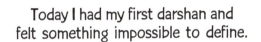

Today I had my first darshan and felt something impossible to define.

The same thing happens to everyone.
Each darshan has the characteristic of being different. No matter if it's your first trip, darshan is a unique and indescribable experience of transformation, although some people have been able to write exactly what happened inside them during their first encounter with Sai Baba.

Sai Baba is all love. The only way to connect ourselves with Him is through love.

Dr. Samuel Sandweis, a Jewish-American psychiatrist, relates in his book "The Spirit and the Mind" that he arrived at the ashram with the fantasy that Baba would immediately recognize him and give him the most divine revelations.

Was that not so?

No! Rather the contrary!

"He made me sit down and wait, I got angry and frustrated, started to think I was crazy for having made this trip expecting an inkling of God. And suddenly, in the moment of most intense pain, he came to me, like the most loving of fathers...."

–Dr. Samuel Sandweis

For each of the millions of visitors, Sai Baba has a special reception. Another American, Joy Thomas, describes her first encounter this way:

"Suddenly, He was standing there, before me, smiling like a thousand suns and asked:'Where are you from?' My voice went to the same kingdom to which my mind had wandered and, though I tried, I was simply not able to say a word. He waited patiently for my answer, asking at last: 'What happened to your voice?' With a soft squeak I managed to say: 'Oh, it's that I love so, Baba'. Baba smiled broadly, as a mother would to a child that no doubt had seen the face of God and whom He had told he loved".   – Joy Thomas

WORK
IS
ADORATION

One who got really angry on her first darshan was Diana Baskin.

Why?

She relates she arrived for the inaugural act of a feminine Sai school. When she got there, they put her way back. She was uncomfortable, sitting on the floor without catching a word of the long conversations in Hindi. That increased her desire to meet Sai Baba, for the situation was not as she had dreamt her first encounter would be.

What happened then?

They went to a patio and ended up in first row. Suddenly Sai came out and went towards her. She thought he would say: "At last you're here, I've waited for you so long!" When he stopped before her, he talked to the people at both sides with a loving smile. He ignored Diana completely.

Sai Baba says He is our mirror. In God, each one is reflected, echoes and reacts. It's hard to understand this through reason. If there are ten thousand people at the darshan, there will be ten thousand different versions of what happened.

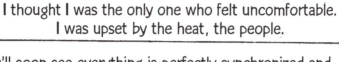

Darshan's therapy

Several hours in advance, people start waiting for Sai Baba's entrance in order to take part in the darshan. Inner work is very intense.

> I thought I was the only one who felt uncomfortable. I was upset by the heat, the people.

> You'll soon see everything is perfectly synchronized and the divine order is present even in the human disorder.

> But so many hours, such a long wait, so much pressing.

> Irritation is an opportunity for inner connection too.

> Why does he only talk to some people?

> Baba has the faculty of giving us what we really need, which doesn't coincide with what we think we need. This isn't paradise, nor a physical place. It's a state of mind.

The darshan is a unique occasion to put before the Lord's feet everything that is preventing us from feeling God at all times. Baba usually repeats:

> *"I don't want your devotion,
> I want your transformation".*

Why are men separate from women at all ashram activities?

Separation keeps our minds from deviating from the objective. Our mind is like a mad monkey: jumping through the branches of the tree of desire. At first, separation is annoying. When you learn to recognize your limitations, you're grateful.

What's that about the mad monkey mind?

All monkeys feel attracted to all they see, especially fruits and colorful things. Their motto is to "take and run". Our mind is more erratic than the monkey's. It jumps from one thought to another, goes from desire to desire, creates a tangle that ends up trapping us.

Can we escape from that net?

Desire catches the mind in the same way hunters trap monkeys.

Hunters put peanuts in a bottle.

The hungry monkey puts his hand in and grabs the peanuts.

When he wants to leave he realizes he can't get his hand out.

The neck is too narrow for his closed fist.

...and he gets desperate thinking there is a trap that doesn't let him take his hand out.

Sai Baba says the world is like a bottle. The situations we live are the bottle's neck. Our desires, the peanuts inside. To be truly free we need to leave out the desires.

"There is no complete freedom without sacrifice nor resignation".

Miracles are my letter of introduction

Sai Baba has demonstrated total control over matter and energy—that is to say, he is omnipotent. He creates anything from naught, or transforms it instantly, cures any illness, even resurrects people. All incomprehensible tasks for the rational mind. His miracles are so striking that many times the result is hard to believe. For those following Sai Baba's life closely, these become habitual. The miracle obliges us to go beyond our mind.

What is a miracle?

For the Royal Spanish Academy it's "an act of divine power, superior to the natural order and human strength".

Sai Baba says that what we call miracles are part of His nature. He says they're his "letter of introduction" so that we pay attention to Him and that He can do the biggest miracle of all: **the transformation of the heart** More than 120 million devotees throughout the planet testify by their own transformations. For example, from selfishness to expansive love, or excessive attachment to an attitude of service...

What is the meaning of the ashes Baba materializes?

The vibhuti is a sacred ash that manifests his divinity. It symbolizes the cycle of life and death in which everything is reduced to ashes at the end. It's the final condition of things. Ashes can't suffer ulterior modifications.

Yet for those receiving them, they have a very profound spiritual significance.

It's an unmistakable sign to abandon desires, burn up passions, ties and temptations in the fire of devotion and service. This makes us pure in thought, word and action.

Sai Baba materializes vibhuti several times a day; about a pound a day, they say.

His ash produces auspicious effects on the physical, mental and spiritual body. It blesses and liberates. There are millions of cases in which the power of faith finds in vibhuti an excellent means of manifestation.

If Sai Baba is a Divine Being, what need does he have to materialize things?

It's a seal of his divinity. His letter of introduction. All that lies beyond our enslaving senses, brings us doubts, fears, unbelief. Baba displays all his battery of miracles to convince us of his divinity.

Magicians make things appear from nothing.

A magician expects the crowd's applause. Sai Baba lives giving all from himself expecting nothing back, except our transformation.

Since Love has no forms, materialization is the evidence of My Love for you. And it's a way for you to be in constant connection with me.

Sai Baba does not materialize objects with the purpose of making money or showing off his powers. He gives them to those he makes them for. It is one of his infinite ways to push us towards investigating the deepest spiritual truths. Though the miracle itself is an inferior event next to the universal revelations it contains, it's a sign more powerful than words. Since men are spiritually lazy, we need to directly witness spectacular events shifting us from the inertia we are in.

All right, but...Why do they have to be material things, like watches, rings, earrings, bracelets?

Those objects work as a permanent line between the person and Sai Baba. A watch or a ring makes him remember God at critical times. They create a very effective sense of security and protection. When you're in problems, you feel that a symbolic bond exists between you and the incarnated divinity in Sai Baba.

First multiplication

Early testimony of his multiplying powers dates from 1940, when he materialized a great deal of a rare fruit of Shirdi origin. It happened like this: he asked for an empty basket, gave it a soft tap and created more than a dozen such fruits. After the devotional chants session, he gave out a fruit to each of the hundreds of people present.

Gordon Ghetty, a devout person from Durban (South Africa) had put his car at the devotees' disposal: he would drive them to the chanting session and back. He would cover enormous distances to do this service. At the time there was a fuel shortage in the country and gas stations were closed on weekends. One Saturday, Ghetty was appalled to find that his fuel tank was almost empty. He had to pick up a number of people and take them home later. He pleaded to Sai Baba. The answer did not take long: so much fuel started gushing out of the tank that he had to put it in bottles. Almost 7 gallons came out. The miracle was repeated on many occasions.

Sai Baba also materializes pens, candy, medicines, statuettes, gold and panchaloka silver (five-metal alloy) jewelry, with emeralds, rubies, pearls, plastic and wooden objects. All of Creation's elements are at his disposal. He just has to wish it and the object is created instantly. A certain time, the editor of an influential Hindu daily did an extensive and arduous interview with the purpose of unmasking him. Sai not only answered all his questions but the journalist was transformed and wrote a book about Sai Baba, *God lives in India*.

Swami, isn't materializing an Omega watch a fraud to the company that makes it?

I assure you there is no such thing. It would be a fraud if I were to transfer the watch from one place to another. I don't transfer objects. I create them completely, whatever you want.

For Australian Howard Murphet he materialized a ten-dollar gold coin minted in 1906 —precisely the same year of his birth. In 1978, the authorities of one of Sai Baba's schools went to visit him at Prashanti Nilayam. To people's surprise, Sai materialized a heavy statue of the god Ganesh for them. He made a gold ring with His portrait surrounded by diamonds for a Madurai merchant. The curiosity: though it had no clockwork, the portrait turned three hundred and sixty degrees every twenty-four hours. Prof. N. Kasturi, who remained with Sai Baba for decades and was his biographer before dying, wrote about the infinite number of materializations Swami had done at river and beach coasts. He created Rama, Krishna and Ganesha statues from the sand.

They passed it on from hand to hand. When they gave it back to him, he made it disappear.

In 1973, he created the same kind of crucifix which Christ died on. Sai Baba was walking with a group of devotees. He stopped in front of a bush, cut two small branches, put one on top of the other and asked Hislop.

What's this, Mr. Hislop?

A cross, Swami.

This shows Christ as he was actually crucified and not how artists and writers imagined. This wood is the same one on which Christ was crucified.

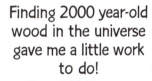

Finding 2000 year-old wood in the universe gave me a little work to do!

On December 1989, Baba called an Argentine group to interview. While he talked to different people, he asked me to give him the watch I had on, a plastic one with a sheer box and straps. He went on talking while he played with my watch, when suddenly he fixed his eyes on me and asked:

Days later, I noticed that the watch's moon phase didn't work. Next time I see him—I thought—I'll ask him to fix it. The following week he called us to interview again. There Sai Baba asked me: "How's your watch doing?" Sitting at His feet I answered: "Fine Swami, thanks". Without saying anything, he put his foot on my left wrist, covering the watch. He left it there for an hour and a half. After the interview, I remembered the watch and looked at it. The moon phase was working normally.

In March of 1991, I married Graciela. Seven days after arriving, Sai Baba gave a speech for the thousands of foreigners who were there. Suddenly, he stopped what he was doing and without getting down from the stage and with the same tone of voice, he looked at me and asks:

Are you from Argentina?

Yes, Swami.

You're on your honeymoon, aren't you? Your wedding ring?

Yes, Swami.

You fight with your wife and make her cry. I know you do.

Yes, Swami.

Don't worry, they're just mental differences. You'll overcome them and always be happy. I'm always going to help you. Right now, she's crying. My heart is crying too.

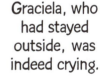

Graciela, who had stayed outside, was indeed crying.

Cures

Diseases and their cures have a close relationship with faith and miracles. These are supernatural events that go beyond natural and scientific laws. They have their root in faith in God or a Man-God. Stories about miraculous cures are as old as the world. Greek mythology boasts famous examples like the Temple of Esculapio, who was god of medicine. There are pilgrimage centers where Men-God relics are kept: Mohammed's hair in Kashmir, Buddha's tooth in Sri Lanka, Jesus' shroud in Turin or Shirdi Sai Baba's relics in Maharashtra. Mecca is associated with curative powers for the Muslims, Lourdes in France and Fatima in Portugal for Christians, Katargama for the Cingalese, Tirupati Venkateswara for the Hindu. Always Sathya Sai Baba has performed incredible cures. His methods are diverse and unknown. Sai Baba "takes" in His body some of His devotees' disease, as a symbol of love and protection. In every case, what cures is His grace, but mainly what cures is the faith in Him or any other form of God.

A famous Hindu scientist, who lived in the States, caught a strange illness that severely weakened him. He was thirty years old at the time. His case was diagnosed as reticular cellular sarcoma of Ewing. By 1964, the disease had expanded all over his body, and metastases were detected in his skull, neck, hip, ribs, kidneys and abdomen. He was given up as a case with no remedy.

At the request of a friend, the following year he gathered strength to travel to India and see Sai Baba. Swami gave him His blessing and asked him to return in 1970. Shortly after, he was cured and went back to work in the U.S.

. . . .

All I did was give him the confidence and willpower to cure himself. It was my abundant love, matched by the devotee's own faith, that finally produced the desired result.

Of his infinite ways to cure, perhaps the most extraordinary is the one in which He himself assumes his devotees illness. "Assuming the disease" means that his body is voluntarily invaded by all kinds of illnesses. He takes them gladly, as part of His mission. In most cases, people are not aware of what he is doing. Sai Baba's body is not the least affected by the diseases he assumes. They never detected ailments in him that, in any other person's case, would have caused some scar, impediments, internal wounds, handicap, etc.

Why doesn't he cure all illnesses? Cure, says Sai Baba, is based on faith and every individual's necessity. For some, having a disease is what they need on their way. Sai Baba is not a healer. He came to raise us spiritually, using all possible means.

In December 1970, after an almost 400-mile trip, Baba and the group accompanying him made a stop at Goa's palace. Swami declined to have dinner and in the morning got up late, which was unusual for Him. Nobody knew he had passed the night with high fever and pain. He got worse during the day. The twenty-four physicians who were consulted diagnosed: acute paracholic appendicitis. Surgery was the only alternative. Sai Baba rejected any kind of medicine or intervention.

Two days later he started to have hiccups, and abscesses led to peritonitis. His death was near. However, the miracle came about on the 10th. Sai Baba got rid of the purulent mass that was storming him in the same way he had assumed it: fast and mysteriously. He recovered and, exactly as planned, delivered a celebrated speech to the crowd that was expecting him.

The most shocking disease-assuming story happened in June 1963, during the Gurupoornima festival. On June 29, Swami loses consciousness and falls heavily to the ground. Two devotees pick him up and put him on a stretcher. His right arm is stiff, his hand hard in a tight fist. His left leg can't be bent; his toes are also rigid. The next morning the picture gets worse: the ailment has already affected his eyes, and Swami can't open his mouth. The adjoin director of Karnataka State, who has come to examine him, reaches a final diagnosis: tuberculosis meningitis. With a scarcely perceptible move, Swami opposes having a lumbar puncture performed. As time goes by, the situation gets worse. He has two heart attacks. On July 3 he suffers another heart attack. For four hours, he seems to oscillate between life and death.

. . . .

In these four hours, I told the flame of life to keep itself alive. I was far away, observing my body from above, unattached and unaltered.

On the morning of the 4th, Sai announced that on Saturday the 6th we would preside at a festival.

On the 6th of July, a big crowd gathers in Prashanti Nilayam, torn by the near loss of their master. Sai is brought down the winding stairs on a sofa. Two people carry him. A third one holds his left foot. His jaw is held up by a scarf around his head. Seeing Sai in such a terrible state, the crowd breaks out in tears, cries and wails. Tension turns to excessive euphoria. For once Prashanti Nilayam's supreme peace gives way to hysteria and confusion. Yet: **Sai Baba gets well before the tens of thousands of people gathered!**

How does he do it? Sitting up on the dais, he asks for a glass of water. He splashes it on himself, just enough to cure his eye, face, leg, shoulder, arm and heart. Immediately, Sai stands up and pronounces a powerful speech. Sai Baba says that every now and then humanity needs to be given this lesson so that faith in God and the power to acknowledge the Divinity will be added to the human faculties.

Death surrenders at his feet

Sai Baba's powers are limited. Like Rama, Krishna and Jesus, he has the faculty to bring those who have already left their bodies back to life. He knows who's who on the spiritual level. No one escapes the eye of God. According to the spiritual aspirant's evolutionary necessities, He answers their prayers and physically presents himself in a visible or invisible way. The devotees of God, in any name or way they adore him, are spiritually comforted by Sai. He is the "divine helper" for the soul's having a transition suited to its needs. In some cases, God determines that a person's passage on Earth is not over and that he must go on. Only then resurrection happens.

For love of his devotees

One day, Swami tells Subama she will live a year longer. She understands and starts serving the poor and the sick in a ritual way. Almost a year later, Sai accepts a devotee's invitation away from Puttaparthi. Before leaving, he says to Subama: "In your last moments, I'll give you Tulsi (leaf from a sacred Hindu tree) water". While he is away, Subama gets worse and dies. The neighbors feel sorry Swami is not there at the time. Subama's body is taken out of the house. When Sai comes back, the village people tell him what has happened.

Remember the story of Lazarus? Brother of Martha and Mary, Lazarus was a sick man whom Jesus loved dearly. Lazarus died during his master's leave. Four days later, when Jesus found out, he went back to Bethany and asked the sisters to show him to the tomb. Then he ordered the stone covering the entrance to be removed. He commended himself to the Almighty and demanded: "Lazarus, come out!" The dead man had his hands and feet bandaged, and his head was covered with a veil. Jesus said: "Untie him and let him walk!" (John 11.1.44.).

In 1953, 60 year-old Mr. V. Radhakrishna repeated the miracle of resurrection. A gastric ulcer had been giving him a hard time for years. A fervent devotee, he decided to go to Prashanti Nilayam in search of a cure. His wife and daughter went with him. As soon as he arrived at the ashram he was put to bed. Knowing of his presence, Sai Baba visited him in his room, but did nothing.

A true trial of faith was beginning for Radhakrishna's wife and daughter.

The following day, both women sat at the bedside waiting for a miracle. There were no signs of life. That day and the next went by without news. Wife and daughter still clung to their faith in Swami. They secretly hoped to see Radhakrishna alive again. In the morning of the third day, the body had gone dark. The smell of decay was penetrating and unbearable. It was suggested to the wife that the body be removed from the ashram. She refused; first she wanted to have Swami's approval. Some of his followers asked him if the body should be burned or sent to the family residence. "We'll see", he answered.

Jesus said: "He who believes in Me, will live although he is dead. And he who believes in Me, will live forever".

Walter and Elsie Cowan, an old and very spiritual California couple, got a telegram in 1971: "Come to Madras immediately. Baba." Though Walter had health problems, they traveled to India and Baba met them on the night of the 23rd. The following day, Walter got worse and passed out. The hotel doorkeeper put him in bed. The doctor who had been to see him declared he was dead. However, he had quickly sent him on an ambulance to a prestigious Bangalore clinic. After examining him carefully, the emergency doctor had also pronounced him dead. A nurse had covered him with a sheet, plugging his nose and ears with cotton. The following morning, Elsie visited Baba to report her husband's death.

· ·

Before Elsie could open her mouth.

Walter is alive. Go back to the hospital. I'll be there at 10.

On the 26th, Walter was declared clinically dead. A relapse surprised him a week later.

Walter is going away.

Twenty days later Walter recovered and was well enough to travel to Whitefield. There, Sai granted him spiritual matrimony. He gave Walter and Elsie clothes and materialized wedding rings for both.

A friend of the Cowans', John Hislop, researched and gathered documentation about what had happened to Walter. The emergency doctor had confirmed he was already dead when he had arrived at the hospital. The nurses and other physicians had said the same. Once back, Walter related that Sai Baba had taken him to a kind of "court of justice" located in another dimension. Arriving, the people there paid tribute to Baba. Swami addressed the being who seemed to be in charge of the place. This one called Walter and showed him an account of his past lives. In it he saw that peace, character and spirituality were his outstanding qualities. Then Baba ordered him to return to his body and complete his mission on Earth. Back in California, Cowan recovered from his diabetes, lived a year and a half longer, looked 15 years younger and was more active than ever. At 80, when he died, Elsie got another telegram from Baba: "Walter has arrived in good shape".

My life is my message

On the threshold of the twenty first century, humanity is constantly manifesting the most negative aspects of the human condition. Selfishness, lust, ire, envy, hate, excessive desires are everyday matters. The rulers and the ruled, teachers and students, parents and children all seem to be submerged in the ignorance that leads us to an "all out" combat. Our efforts seem to aim more at personal survival than the quest for happiness.

In our uncontrolled run for temporal success, we've fallen into a state of spiritual "comfort". We look outside for what is inside of us. The result is calamitous. Anybody in their right mind can see that the way we're going is wrong. The planet needs direction.

"After long quests here and there, in temples and churches, on land and skies, you have finally come back to complete the circle you came from and reach your own soul. This is your own essence, the Self, the ultimate reality of life: our true nature".

Man had moved away from his path and stopped feeling love for God, when men of good will from all the world raised their prayers to the One. They acknowledged the decline of rectitude. They were hurt to see injustice proudly walking. They pleaded for protection of the good and for the destruction of the evil in men. Sathya Sai Baba is the answer to those prayers.

Contemporaneous leaders think one thing, say another and do a third. The same mistake is repeated in homes and schools. The result is obvious: confusion. Confusion brings pain. Pain embodies the search of pleasure as a palliative and this results in more pain.

...His life is his message. One of the main aspects of his teachings is the coherence between thought, word and action. Every year millions of people pass by his *ashram*. Not all are devotees. There's scientists, journalists and skeptics as well who are willing to find the signs that will allow them to prove he is a fraud. Ever since his life went public, nobody has been able to certify anything about him that does not correspond to what he preaches. Every day for seventy years, he has given unequivocal answers about his Divinity, even to those who have gone to criticize or unmask him.

Total awareness of His mission

When Sai Baba was twenty, his older brother was worried about the growing number of followers who approached Him. Sathya writes him a letter saying:

"I have the task to nurture all humanity and assure their lives are full of beatitude. I have the commitment to lead those who have gone away from the right path to goodness and save them. I'm dedicated to a "job" I love: to end the suffering of the poor and give them what they lack. Those who are devoted to Me must treat the joys and sorrows, gains or losses with equality. I will never abandon those who give themselves up to Me..."

Sai Baba does not bring an original or new message. He says nothing that Jesus, Buddha, the prophet Mohammed, Moses, Rama, Krishna or Guru Nanak haven't already said. But a seal distinguishes him: **he is alive.** We can experience him; try him. His message comes straight from him. There is no spiritual hierarchy to connect with Sai Baba. No categories, nor any kind of distinctions. Before the eyes of God, we are all equal. Sai Baba repeats: "Between my devotees and I there are no mediators. Our connection is heart to heart".

I have come to light Love's lamp in the hearts, so that it may shine day after day with great splendor. Not to publicize any creed, sect or cause. Nor to collect followers for any doctrine. I have no plans for luring disciples to Me. I have come to tell you about this Unitary Universal faith, this Divine Principle, this way to Love. This obligation to Love...

Did anyone predict Sai's advent?

In Revelation (Apocalypse, Saint John, Chap. 19, V. 11), the Lord of Lords appears riding a white horse. He starts his mission after Israel's rebirth. His name is "truth", and, Sathya means "truth" in the Sanskrit language.

Has anyone else announced him?

Volume 13 of "The Ocean of Light" says: "His hair will be abundant. He will be neatly shaved. He will have a mole on one of his cheeks. His clothes will be flame colored. With a small body. Young lady legs. All the precepts of every religion will dwell in his heart from birth. He will make light-weight presents. He will take things out of his body and mouth. He will live 95 or 96 years.

Sai Baba announced he will leave his body at ninety six, exactly in 2020.

In 1976, Dr. R. K. Karanjía, editor of a Marxist-oriented Bombay paper, published the interviews he had done with Sai. Typically materialistic, he intended to prove Sai Baba was a fraud. Aware or not, Karanjía was the tool God used to erase the doubts of millions of people all over the world. He would later recognize that Sai Baba had answered even the questions he had never got around to asking. Finally, he recognized his Divinity.

Skeptics ask why God would assume a human form.

What is his purpose?

To make it evident to man that God lives inside of him. The avatar takes a human form and behaves as such for humanity to discover its relation with the Divinity, at the same time he rises to divine heights to aspire reaching God.

To unite humanity in one unique family, establishing the divine within each being. Once this is done, love will overcome.

Short stories, anecdotes and jokes are his teaching method.

Are we headed for destruction? Will salvation only come after a war?

Evil will be eliminated before that catastrophe. I have come to raise human consciousness above the ire, hate and violence.

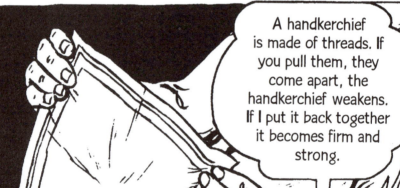

A handkerchief is made of threads. If you pull them, they come apart, the handkerchief weakens. If I put it back together it becomes firm and strong.

Same thing happens to humanity. Love holds you together like the billions of threads in the cloth. Devotion unites them to God.

"Thousands of lamps are lit, but electric energy is one. The full moon is reflected on several pools of water, but it's the same for everybody".

Is there a difference between God and man?

God is man and man is God.
All of us have something of Him, the "divine spark". The difference is that I'm aware of this and you're not.

Can't you help humanity by controlling the natural forces and preventing disasters?

If I interfere in the problems all the action and evolution will immediately stop. I prefer to elevate people so that they understand the truth of the spiritual laws. This will relate them to nature again and sow the good.

Sai Baba's answer was concrete. However, who wouldn't like everything to change in the blink of an eye? Who hasn't dreamt at some point about magic solutions to the world's wrongs? More than one has, for sure. Even John Lennon sung his hope in "Imagine". But only God knows what the best medicine for us is. And there's no doubt it'll be the perfect treatment for healing the soul.

Sai Baba sees us all alike. The rich and the poor have the same soul. The poor man's heart is capable of loving as much as the rich man's. To God, all are his children, without distinction. However, in everyday living, some want to have more, often at the others' expense. And these want to stop being poor at the expense of the first.

Were you successful in your task with the powerful?

Why?

I haven't reached them as a "class", but to the extent I have contacted them individually, the results are pretty encouraging.

The rich powerful class is hard to transform. The poor are more cooperative. They understand, help, have a higher concept about my plans and ideas.

How would you solve the conflict between the rich and the powerful and the poor and weak?

How can you unite both classes?

Forming one sole and cooperative brotherhood with equality, without competence or conflict and by truth and love. It consists of uniting them on a common basis. The rich live isolated lives. The poor too, but under different conditions.

I do it in many subtle ways. I try to break the barriers between wealth and poverty and create a sense of equality.

In Prashanti Nilayam, people of all classes live and work together. They do domestic chores side by side, without distinctions. The rich don't receive any special treatment. They live, eat, work, sleep and do their religious activities the same as the poor. All share the ashram's austerities.

Peace of mind

Sai Baba explains to Karanjía: *"In spite of our rigid discipline, powerful industrialists and businessmen live here. Why? Because they obtain peace of mind that goes beyond the physical community. They can't buy or obtain that peace through wealth or power on Earth. This way we open a world of spiritual treasures to them that they can only receive detaching themselves from the necessities and material comforts".*

Peace of mind creates a sense of companionship, a brotherhood of giving and receiving between the rich and poor. Those who have too much feel the need to resign their unnecessary possessions, while those who have very little see their necessities fulfilled. Sai Baba's objective is that we understand that, in spiritual terms, all humanity belongs to the same class, race or religion. The divine principles derive from a Unique God. This fundamental unity manifests by direct contact with the spiritual realities.

For his political ideas or because a growing spiritual yearning was arising in him as the interview went on, Karanjía wanted to go beyond the rich and poor theme.

To the poor all this comes as a simple and welcome preaching, nothing to lose and a lot to gain. Why don't the rich react? Haven't they got a lot to lose with this philosophy?

The rich must only detach themselves of their false values if they want grace. There's no solution if people continue to be slaves of the wealth-poverty materialism. I try to convert their minds and hearts so that they have spiritual values and truths.

"Which man is richer:
he who has more necessities, and therefore more worries and
difficulties, or he who is satisfied with life's most elementary
necessities, therefore has very few desires and is comparatively
happy?"

"Spiritual and not material satisfaction is what makes life worthwhile. Living without desires brings divinity to man, and those who look for My Grace must get rid of all desire and lust. Wealth provides a fatal tendency: the source and cause of human slavery. Desire to raise the living standards is never satisfied. It leads us to multiply our necessities which causes more troubles and frustrations. Stress the quality not the standard of living; have high thoughts and a simple way of life".

Science and spirituality

We humans have a strong tendency to believe what we see and reject what escapes our limited comprehension. Erroneously, we leave out what lies beyond our understanding. Reason exacerbates the mind. "Seeing is believing" is humanity's dogma. The spiritual way works backwards: "Believing is seeing". Submission to reason's discretion has created antagonism between science and spirituality. Such rivalry is pure illusion. There is no science without God. What does Sai Baba say about science and spirituality?

"How can science, tied as it is to a physical and materialistic point of view, investigate transcendental phenomena beyond its reach or comprehension? Science must limit its research to things concerning the human senses, since spirituality transcends the senses. What science has found out till now is just a fraction of the cosmic phenomenon".

Science is developing all the time. Yesterday's metaphysics is today's physics.

It still remains blind to the vast invisible world of the consciousness. The fact it's constantly changing proves its incapacity to investigate the supreme truth. Some time ago they affirmed the atom was indivisible. Today they divide it. They still ignore the realities of the atom's and its elements' divine force".

"Science is a mere firefly compared with the light and splendor of Sun. It's true it can investigate, discover and collect much data on Nature and its material functions, and employ it to develop mundane things, but..."

"... spirituality rules over the cosmic field where science has no place. That's why some scientific discoveries are useful and others are disastrous".

A lot of scientists say "nothing can be created from nothing". You deny that law with your transcendental way of controlling cosmic energy and producing supernatural powers. Can you explain this?

That "nothing can be created from nothing" is all right if we're dealing with the limited world of science. It doesn't apply to the transcendental and spiritual field. In this last field, anything can be created by the supreme will. All that exists can be made to disappear and all that doesn't exist can be made to appear. Material laws don't apply to the divinity. To me there's no mystery. What I want, happens. What I order materializes.

Karanjía turned out to be a thorough investigator. Maybe then he didn't know his "journalistic sting" was the most efficient way to draw definitions from Sai on points he had never touched in public.

When you say God exists in all of us, isn't it pure escapism by chance? How can God be so insecure?

All of India's scriptures asseverate that God is present in each one of us. It's the only thing that manifests and is common to everything and everybody.
It rules the whole universe. It's the divinity. Outside of that there is **NOTHING**.

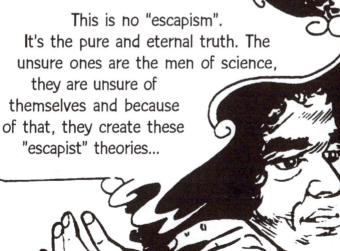

This is no "escapism".
It's the pure and eternal truth. The unsure ones are the men of science, they are unsure of themselves and because of that, they create these "escapist" theories...

They say there's no life on the Moon.

At the same time they say that all matter consists of moving atoms. Isn't the Moon a conglomerate of these same moving atoms? Then, how can there be no life? Each substance is composed of atoms, electrons, neutrons and protons, all moving continuously. This energy too is God. There are no human beings lacking God. To say that God is not in man is like affirming that there are no atoms on the Moon. God is a tiny particle in the tiniest of particles and a great mass in the greatest of masses.

"With such haste to achieve money, fame, success and pleasures, we lose the compass and find ourselves adrift. A moment of pleasure is followed by one of pain and so on. The cobweb traps and prevents us from going on the genuine path".

Which path is that?

When man turns to the inside to realize his true self, then God manifests before him. Self-realization is realization of God. Discovering that you are more than body and mind. The being, that is omnipresent, omnipotent and omniscient, exists within you. When you understand this, you're already on your way.

As a body, mind and soul, you are a mere passing illusion. Now and always you are actually existence, knowledge and beatitude. You are the God of this **UNIVERSE**.

You have the capacity to break the slavery of the body-mind relation and broaden your being to include the Earth, the suns and planets. The entire cosmos inside yourselves!

No body or mind or brain matter. No given desire, nor its objective. Beyond all this there's you, the being, the soul, God...

All these things are simply external manifestations of the inner God. Everything is inside you. Look for it. Discover it. Get to know it. Realize it. You'll realize the world is not an object of desire.

If we break the body-mind relation...Do we die? Is dying a liberation? What is dying and living? What are the body and mind good for?

You don't need to get rid of the body and mind. They're like the fan and the lightbulb. We have to use them. But we shouldn't forget that the electric current makes them useful things. Without power they would have no purpose.

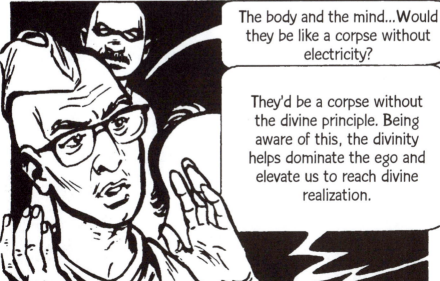

The body and the mind...Would they be like a corpse without electricity?

They'd be a corpse without the divine principle. Being aware of this, the divinity helps dominate the ego and elevate us to reach divine realization.

Sai Baba only preaches the **Religion of Love** for all. He believes it is the only thing that can integrate the human race in one brotherhood of man under God's paternity. He only knows one language: that of the heart, which is beyond the mind and the intellect and relates man to man and man to God. Sai Baba wants to build a humanity without religious, class or any other barriers.

Wouldn't you enter into conflict with the established religions because of this?

My quest is to establish the universal religion, which believes in only one God as the creator that all the religions teach. Nobody should give up their religion or deity, but by it adore the only God in common. I've come to vindicate the fact that each one is his faith.

"When we feel humanity is a universal empire of love, we'll feel the whole world is our family".

Hindus, Muslims, Jews, Catholics, Buddhists, Shintoists, Taoists, Sikhs, Jainists live together in his ashram...all practicing what, to Sai Baba, is the only religion, one of Love in an ambiance of marked tolerance.

The lotus flower conveys a deep meaning for the spiritual seeker. The plant is rooted in the mud, the stem surrounded by water, the flower rising over the surface, blooming in the air, receiving the sun's rays. The spiritual aspirant is born on this land, lives surrounded by the waters of life. Like the lotus he has to strive to go out of the water and further on to catch the sun's rays which are in his own heart. Although it lives in the water, the lotus stays dry, waterproof. The aspirant needs to practice detachment and resignation. The lotus is never contaminated by the water in which it lives, no matter how muddy the environment.

The central column of the lotus is an ancient symbol representing man's ancient aspiration to reach enlightenment. Its flame is represented in the lotus middle and signifies the glow of Supreme Knowledge. Three concentric circles surround the pillar's base. The most external one represents the eternal effort we make to obtain transitory things. The other two represent the kinds of hate men must overcome: the one caused by offenses and the one coming from the frustration of our own desires. When ire, hate and desires leave our mind, we enter into the lotus's open space: equanimity.

Before the **Om** listen to the primordial sound echoing in your hearts, at the same time as in the heart of the universe.

Before the **Buddhist** wheel remember the wheel of cause and effect, of action and destiny; the wheel of Dharma moves them all.

Before the **Zoroastrian** fire offer all your bitterness and resurge from it magnificent, majestic and divine.

Before the **Cross** cut the **I** sensation at the root and let your ego die on the Cross; you'll achieve immortality.

Before the moon, **Muslim** stars and the star of David. Like the stars, never move away from the crescent and establish yourself on the immovable faith.

The purpose of all religions, faiths and creeds is the mind's sublimation to guarantee man's freedom and bring happiness to society, which man is part of. Some religions tried to press holy ideals into the hearts of men, but their selfish desires for power and success didn't allow man to bloom and grow. Many religions encouraged torture and persecution; instead of uniting, they separated.

When people don't realize that the human family is an indivisible unity, they start hating their neighbor and the other religions.

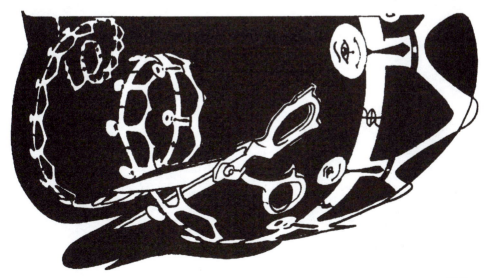

Sai's toolbox

Sai Baba does not do the inner work that behooves each one of us to do. He gives us the tools to successfully carry out the crusade for personal transformation. A difficult crusade in which we can be victorious if we incorporate into our daily habits the three instruments of the "Divine toolbox": devotion, education and service.

Devotion

According to the dictionary, devotion means "celerity to submit to God's will." Sai Baba perfects the concept; he says: "When the mind is cleaned of all sediment or impurity and noble feelings are cultivated, then Wisdom's Vision can come out and Creation is perceived in all its splendor."

"If there are to be no flowers, no buds will show.
And if no buds show, there will be no fruits either.
If you don't carry out an activity dedicated to the Lord, that is
to say an activity free of desires, devotion will not arise and
without devotion wisdom will not dawn".

Devotional practices are an efficient method for finding the connecting source with the Superior. With perseverance, step by step, man climbs the divine ladder that takes him to God.

Sai Baba says devotion is like a garland made with eight flowers.

MEDITATION

TRUTH

EQUANIMITY

NONVIOLENCE

PATIENCE & TOLERANCE

CONTROL OF THE SENSES

COMPASSION FOR BEINGS

ASCETIC SPIRITUAL PRACTICE

"Worshipping God with these eight flowers can lead you to gain His complete Grace. Rather than worshipping him through the flowers of Nature, that wither and lose their fragrance, worship God with the flowers of your virtues".

God is omnipresent. We know, but it's hard for us to experience it; to feel it each moment, action, place. Our crazed way of life frequently makes us forget there is anything more to this world. Something more transcendent. We run wildly after passing pleasures, wanting more money, more status, a better car, a bigger house, better clothes. We hardly ever want to **"feel God better"**. Devotion is the strategy we have to go from the unreal to the real, from darkness to light, from death to immortality. Meditation is one of the devotional tools Sai Baba recommends.

"We are three people: the one we think we are, the one others think we are and the one we really are. Meditation helps to leave aside the first two".

Meditation helps to recapture consciousness of unity with the Creator, to control the mind, the senses and the body. We need this control in order to reach disinterest in the fruits of our action. Disinterest is linked to the genuine love for all beings and the desire to serve. This love leads to self-realization.

Meditation in the Light

Sai Baba recommends this technique. It consists of meditating in a fixed time and place. In the morning, before starting our daily activities. At night, before going to bed. We look for a comfortable position, sitting on a blanket or cushion, on the floor or a chair. Our backs must be straight and our bodies relaxed. In front of us, we place lit candles. Next to them, if we want, we can put an image with the form of God we venerate. We repeat the Om three times and then give ourselves up to God so He will guide us.

The first stage is to feel we are in the Light. For that, we stare at the lit candle till closing our eyes. The light is fixed between the eyebrows. Then, we keep pace with breathing rhythm. The easiest way is to observe our respiration. This way the process gets slower and quieter. When we inhale, our respiration produces the sound "So", meaning God. Exhaling, it sounds like "Ham". Synchronized breathing makes up the "So Ham" mantra. God and I are One.

The next step is the stage called "The Light is within Me". Marking the respiratory rhythm, we slowly start feeling the Light approaching and penetrating us between the eyebrows, illuminating the entire head. From there, it slowly goes down to rest on the heart, which opens up like a flower, petal by petal, to receive the Divine Clarity.

The last step is called "I am the Light". Once installed in our hearts, it floods the senses, and commutes to every part of the body.

Let my legs always lead to places where I can do good deeds.

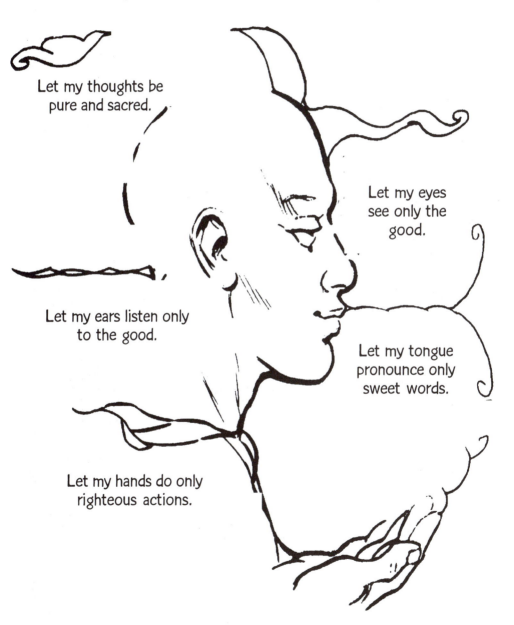

Let my thoughts be pure and sacred.

Let my eyes see only the good.

Let my ears listen only to the good.

Let my tongue pronounce only sweet words.

Let my hands do only righteous actions.

Immediately after, we radiate the Light where we meditate to family, friends, our city, the country, the continent, the world and finally bathe the whole Universe in light. It's important to send light to the people we consider our enemies; and moreover, strive to acknowledge that they possess the same divine spark that lives in us. Once done it's time to conclude the meditation. These are the following steps:
• Visualize again the Divine Light in the heart,
• Ask for "all the beings of all worlds to be eternally happy".
• Thank God for the meditation,
• Slowly open your eyes trying to cherish the peace attained.

Devotional song

Singing is another fun and useful way to expand devotion. All mankind's religions and cultures recognize that song from the heart elevates us to a more sublime emotional and spiritual state. We sing at baptisms, initiations, weddings and funerals: millenary and contemporary melodies, fast and slow, with or without instruments, coral and individual.

Sai Baba teaches the efficiency that devotional song (bhajans) produces. He inspires devotees to sing to all the forms and names of God. The bhajans generally name Jesus, Buddha, Allah, Jehovah, Krishna, Rama, Zoroaster, Guru Nanak, Brahma, Vishnu, Shiva, Shirdi Sai Baba, Sathya Sai Baba...

"The bhajans are the soap and water for cleaning the mind of bad thoughts. Always keep the name of the Lord on your lips and you'll see that all thoughts of envy and hate disappear from your hearts. Get the maximum benefit from the years that have been assigned to you".

Repeating the name of God

"If I take a grain of sugar, put it on my fingertip and say: 120 million grains like this make up a mountain, you will still not know what a mountain is. To realize your experience, you need to go straight to it, approaching it as much as you can. The same thing happens with God", says Sai Baba.

Prayer is the first tool for those who want direct contact with God. Prayer is the common denominator of all religions. In the Hindu religion, there is an instrument to help you pray and encourage the practice: the *japamala*. It's a rosary with 108 beads, each representing an attribute of God. Sai Baba recommends its periodic use as a way of going deep into one's own religion.

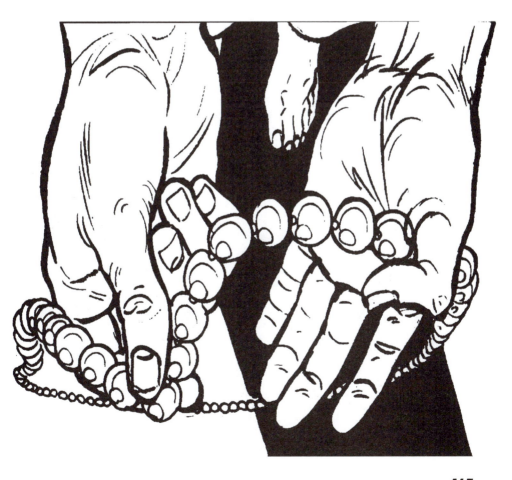

Sai Education

We can cross the water like fish. We can fly like birds, even reach the Moon. But every day we find it harder to live together on Earth like brothers. We have become our worst enemies. To change this discouraging picture, Sai Baba tells us we have to transform education, where we form those who will govern in the future.

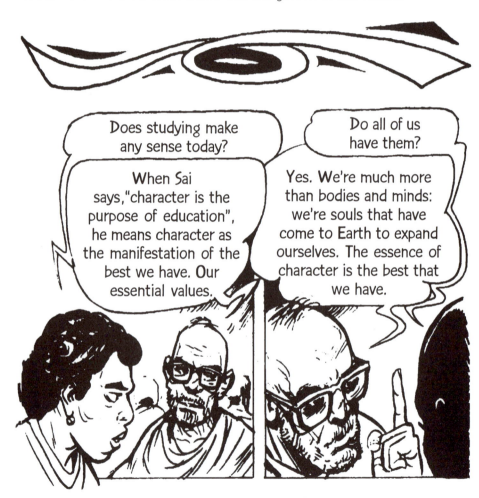

Education is more than attaining a way of life: it is aimed at developing an integral man, with deep awareness of his values and an interest in active participation in the improvement of human community.

Sathya Sai Baba Program of Education in Human Values

Sai Baba gave teachers a tool that could be used in elementary schools all over the world, transcending surface differences of religion, color, etc. He designed a program with the objective of developing the children's deepest values, those which express the different levels of their personality:

Level	Expressed by	Value
physical	actions	rectitude
emotional	emotions	peace
mental	thoughts	truth
intuitive	intuitions	love
spiritual	total being	nonviolence

"The best action we can do is the right action and this will show rectitude. The best thought manifests the truth. When our emotions are in balance we perceive peace. Through our highest intuition we transmit that powerful energy we know as love. And when this love is universal, the spiritual level starts working and nonviolence emerges".

Sai Baba has founded hundreds of elementary and secondary schools throughout India. They reflect this educational conception which seeks the global development of body, mind and spirit. In addition, Sai Baba has founded three universities. In these institutions, the students don't have to pay anything at all. They receive a secular and spiritual education of the highest quality imaginable. They count with the latest teaching equipment. Students get up at 5 A.M. and practice *hatayoga*, do some sports, sing devotional songs, and meditate. Once physically, mentally, emotionally and spiritually harmonized, they have breakfast and then continue with classes. Those who study near Prashanti Nilayam and Whitefield go to darshan to see Sai Baba.

1200 students go to the University of Prashanti Nilayam; 1000 men and 1000 women attend the two Whitefields. There you can study to obtain a master's degree and a doctorate in biosciences, math, physics, chemistry, electronics, scientific computing, business administration, finance, commerce, optics, English, literature, philosophy ...The rigor goes further than the teaching and the mere transmission of data . To Sathya, the message of a knowledge that is preached but not practiced is incoherence . The professors of

Sathya's schools lead exemplary lives. It's not accidental that one of the most important subjects at the Sai Schools is called **Conscience**–obligatory in all fields of study. This way students can learn Sai's message in detail, study the different religions and their sacred texts to acknowledge the Unity which exists in all of them and bring human values closer to society. Besides what they study, students practice another fundamental subject they will apply no matter what career they choose: **social service**. They prepare and serve more than 15,000 meals to the needy, and do humanitarian and sanitation chores in adopted villages.

If a student fails, he only influences himself, but if a professor does not accomplish his duty, hundreds of students will suffer the consequences.

At present students cannot define the basis of their lives, nor whatever is of importance. They do not have that patriotism born of love for their nation, nor the devotion to God that inspires a spirit of sacrifice. They seem to have lost confidence. From this loss off confidence come most of the ills affecting the world. So, Sai Baba insists:

Do not use your privileges as a bowl for begging some reward for any task. Make appropriate use of your edecation to give service to your people and so lead a noble life.

- "Cling to truth and righteousness so as to sustain life".

- "Education is the closest relative when one is far from home".

- "To make humankind compassionate is the culmination of education's purpose".

- "Without self knowledge and control of the emotions, nobody may be considered educated".

- "It is imperative to purify whatever is hidden so that whatever is visible may flourish".

- "To enter into Heaven, a person must be transformed into an innocent child".

Love everyone, serve everyone

The third element of connection and inner transformation that Sai Baba defines as "the direct way to God" is disinterested service to the community.

Men are like empty water jars. Through prayer and chants we fill ourselves with beatitude.

Through daily practice of human values, we express our essence and transform ourselves.

Pouring out our disinterested service over society, we empty ourselves so that the divine grace may fill us again. Filling and emptying ourselves is the process that leads to enlightenment.

Thousands of years ago, spiritual seekers needed to get away from civilization. Today there are thousands of ways to become enlightened. Street kids, unsheltered elderly, terminal patients, the poor—all these are His ways. Sai Baba asks: "How can God appreciate your meditation when there's someone next to you who is in agony, who you haven't treated piously, who you're not making any effort for?"

When we think about service, we automatically think of charity and welfare. Giving away money we have to spare, donating clothes we no longer use, giving the toys our children have left... We also think about the actions of Mother Teresa, Albert Schweitzer, Saint Francis, Gandhi...

How can I do service? Where?

With faith, surrender and self-confidence, every second of your life is an opportunity to do it. It's an attitude, a way of life. A disposition that works like the automated teller machines, 24 hours a day 365 days a year.

"Live together with the people searching for the opportunity to help, but have the name of God on your lips and the form of God in mind's eye".

Life has become vertiginous. Speed compels us to automate actions that are really services. Any job we might do, if we do it with the right attitude, without egotistic thoughts, is a service. How can you tell an attitude of service from a mechanical one? Tiny as it may be, any act given up to God with the awareness that He is the doer and we are the instruments is a true service.

Every morning, when we get up, the first thing we do is brush our teeth. We do it out of habit. Do we ever think we are doing a service to our bodies?

"The body is the temple where God has installed. By brushing our teeth, we keep them healthy. With healthy teeth, we chew correctly. Good chewing betters digestion. A quiet digestion avoids us pain. Without pain, we feel better to serve. Brushing our teeth is a service".

When we help a blind person cross the street, do we do it out of habit or as a service? When we give our seat to an old person or a pregnant woman, are we aware we are serving or do we think we're well educated?

Doing service
daily acts

Small examples of everyday deeds that could be a great service if we give them up to God. As they come up, write them down...

- Breathing
- Being a good son or daughter, father, mother, brother...
- Being a good fellow worker
- Smiling to your neighbors
- ....
- ....
- ....
- ....
- ....
- ....
- ....
- ....
- ....
- ....
- ....
- ....
- ....
- ....
- ....
- ....
- ....
- ....

Service is made up of a series of essential qualities, common to all human beings. The main one is Love. Without it, any action we perform will be a service without food or a blanket. When love accompanies every act, its use opens the heart's "ear", without which we could hardly listen to another's real needs.

"A man strolls by the side of a river. While he walks he sees a dying fish. Full of love and compassion for the fish, he picks him up and takes him with him.
'He must be very cold', he thinks as he walks into his house. Without losing time, he lays him down next to the chimney. He gives him a hot cup of coffee. Obviously, the fish can't drink it.
He's dead".

Service inspires gratitude to our four mothers:

Divine Mother. The Creator's feminine energy aspect. It must be venerated as the Giver of all kinds of life. You honor her by service.

Mother Nature. This loving mother allows us to feed ourselves, grow, heal. You honor her by caring for her. This millennium's advanced ecological awareness is what will allow us to reverse the processes of deterioration that man has caused to Mother Nature's generosity.

Mother Country. We all have a debt of gratitude to society.

We owe her our ability to study, work, grow, be somebody...If we don't serve society, who are we going to serve? You honor her by working above all differences (ethnic, religious, social...)

Biological Mother. "The sweet divinity in human life derives from maternal love. In the protection and breeding of the child there is a spirit of sacrifice that makes maternity precious", says Sai Baba. You honor her by constant gratitude for giving us life and teaching us to love.

Genuine and pure service is done with total detachment. This means serving without waiting for the results; ceasing to be interested in the fruits of our actions. He who acts with humility, love in his heart, softness in his voice and sweetness in his doing is a true server. The-end-of-the century challenge is to provide relief to the needy, comforting them: cheering up hearts hurt by a lack of love. This is the only way the world will achieve peace.

The river flows permanently. Trees give fruits.
Cows give milk. They do it for others.
They claim no reward or recognition for their acts.

The great lesson that derives from serving is surprising: the most benefited is not the served but the server. *"Take one step towards Me and I'll take a hundred towards you"*, says Sai Baba. Speculative rules don't work with service: service is opening your heart, giving love in the way each situation requires.

Doing service necessary qualities

Make yourself a list like the one below and try to remember the basic elements of service. As they come up, write them down:

• Love
• Compassion
• Ability
• Detachment
• ....
• ....
• ....
• ....
• ....
• ....
• ....
• ....
• ....
• ....
• ....
• ....
• ....
• ....
• ....
• ....
• ....
• ....
• ....

Service is love in action

Service
of feeding

Sai Baba does not exhaust His mission with preaching. He puts His Mission into practice. He clears up all the doubts through practice. He says what he thinks and does what he says. He personifies coherence. His labor is enormous. Every day thousands of indigents crowd to receive a serving of food prepared by Sai Baba's devotees. Many times, He postpones appointments to personally serve the meal. Students from his schools also serve more than 15,000 daily helpings to the poor. Throughout India and the world, Sai's devotees do this service feeding those who cannot obtain food for themselves.

Village
adoption

In India, devotees form groups to adopt rural villages, where tolerable hygienic and sanitary conditions do not exist. There is no drinkable water. People are frequent victims of all kinds of parasites, virus and bacteria. Servers do cleaning and maintenance chores, teach trades, organize medical camps, teach crafts and give educational support.

Teaching trades

Sai's servers operate trade schools so the disabled and the poor may find some working occupation. The servers in Bombay may be the most active of all. They have eighteen institutions for the blind. There, students take carpentry, tailoring and candle fabrication courses for free. Study lasts from three to four years, then students are helped to find work.

Other Sai institutions teach adults for free. One of them has 550 students. There, with volunteer help, the children teach their parents to read and write. In another poor neighborhood of the city, three doctors, a dentist and ten volunteers opened up a free clinic that serves more than 600 people a week. These actions are repeated around the world. Millions of people have understood **that service is the backbone of the Sai message.**

We don't share our money. All they need is to share our love and care. We identify ourselves with their unhappiness. This is the only way we can work properly.

I treat myself as if I were illiterate, or a cancer patient. I want to understand them so as to serve them right. I want them to feel as happy as I am.

Medical
service

God made us in his image. We are his children. However, the ambition and selfishness that humanity suffers has turned a rich and generous planet like ours into an empire of inequities. This social corrosion extends to health care. "Health care is a right for all and not a gift for just a few", teaches Sai Baba. He founded a series of hospitals throughout India, completely free to assist the needy. Among them, the **Hospital of Super Medical Specialties stands out**. This hospital has a miraculous story, which serves as an unequivocal sign that Sai's Divine Hand controlled the whole building process.

The story begins with a young and vigorous American businessman, Isaac Tigrett. Owner of the famous **Hard Rock Cafe**, Tigrett feels his role at the head of the business is coming to an end. When he is still doubting whether he can sell it at the price he wants, someone offers to buy it for much more than he thought to get. Since Isaac's devotion for Sai dates from many years back, he soon realizes that the buyer as well as the price are His Will. So he decides to donate much of the profit as a work of service. "Let's do a model hospital", says Sai Baba and puts him at the head of the project.

On November 23 of 1990, Sai Baba delivers a speech in which he announces that the following year, on the same date, he will open the hospital. The announcement causes wonder, and many are full of doubts. Tigrett himself recalls that he was also assaulted by doubt during that year. On November 22, a few minutes after the inauguration, the first open heart operation takes place there.

It was built on a terrain of almost 180 acres. More than 3000 people worked on it. The work was directed by a prestigious English architect, who specialized in hospitals and temples. The medical structure was organized by the famous American Hospital Corporation. The building's geometry echoes Arabic and Islamic forms. It is painted in soft colors which gives it greater luminosity and beauty. The rooms are located on the curves, downplaying the long corridors. Ample gardens next to the rooms allow the patients to keep in touch with the external world. The building has a residential complex for physicians, nurses and employees in addition to houses for the patients' relatives. Few U.S. and European hospitals possess so much latest-generation medical equipment. The hospital has capacity for 300 patients. They do heart operations and heart, kidneys, and cornea transplants...Since 1996 it has had oncological and pneumological services, and 450 beds. Till now they have done 4000 surgical interventions. In international medical congresses they estimated that its infection rate is 0.8%, with a mortality lower than 2%—among the lowest in the world. The **Hospital of Super Medical Specialties'** inspiring action influenced the opening of many free medical units all over India.

Sri Sathya Sai Hospital of Super Medical Specialties

Water
for everybody

In 1993, when Sai Baba turned sixty eight, he was asked what he wanted for his seventieth birthday. *"Drinking water for 700 villages"*, he answered. Puttaparthi, Sai's hometown, is one of thousands scattered throughout the state of Andra Pradesh. The region suffers terrible droughts. A great number of people must walk up to three miles a day to get water from a well, under a burning sun, carrying heavy jars on their heads. The water draw has up to 75 times more arsenic than normal, due to contamination of the soil.

More than 13 thousand people work day and night digging holes on the dry riverbanks, opening canals from the existing irrigation ducts, building reservoirs for the summer, drilling where the underground courses run, installing more than 1250 miles of pipes and installing tanks holding 40,000 gallons each.

Away
with fluorine

The enduring people of Andra Pradesh consume not only an enormous amount of arsenic but fluorine as well. Ingesting big quantities of this element produces "fluorosis". The ailment begins to manifest in the teeth with discoloration. Then it spreads to the skeleton, causing strong pain and finally bone malformations. Analyzing this problem, scientists of the Sai Baba University invented and built a water processing plant that chemically filters fluorine. The purifying filter turned out to be a success, and by Sai's grace was installed in numerous villages. This project's importance and magnitude attracted the Indian government and UNICEF, which helped to install the tanks.

The world at His feet

In seventy years, Sai Baba has left India just once. When he was young, he visited Oriental Africa for a few days. His whole life has gone by in the "ex" rural village of Puttaparthi. However, more than 120 million people throughout the world recognize Him as a divine incarnation. Even in the Islamic countries or Socialist states, his devotees form groups following His teachings. Aware that His counsel leads to the right path, He has consented to the creation of a worldwide organization carrying His name. Sai Centers worldwide do devotional, educational and service activities. Sai Baba has prohibited fees for any of the activities. One significant feature is the fact that there are no spiritual hierarchies. This particular path consists in preaching what you think and practicing what you preach, without telling others what to do and how to do it. The climate which vibrates at the Sai Centers is of a high luminous intensity, inspiring and refreshing, elevating and impacting.

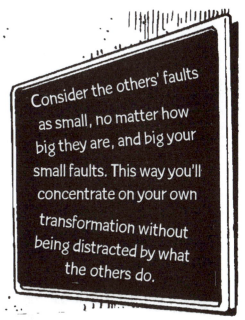

Consider the others' faults as small, no matter how big they are, and big your small faults. This way you'll concentrate on your own transformation without being distracted by what the others do.

The unforgettable party

On November 23, 1995, Sai Baba celebrated his seventieth birthday. More than two million people, from more than 140 countries, gathered at Puttaparthi. All were fed for free, all were housed. The party included Sai's and several of his devotees' inspiring speeches. The celebration included the flag parade of the countries that comprise the Sai Organization; Sai Geeta, Sai's elephant, lavishly dressed up; eminent dancers; and performances by elementary school children. A helicopter flew overhead, casting out candy, messages and garlands. For several days, a cultural program including musical concerts and traditional Indian dancing cheered the afternoons. At the same time, the Sixth Sai Baba World Conference took place. During the exhausting days, tens of thousands of world delegates discussed ways to **raise humanity's consciousness** through devotion, education and service.

"Very soon, there will be a Sai Center on every street", Sai Baba said some years ago. Conclusions at the end of the conference estimate His admonition will come about sooner than we think. The visual postcards of the conference and the birthday still tickle in my heart. People sleeping wherever they could, even out in the open. Millions of humans waiting hours on end to see the Avatar. Men, women and children who sacrificed their comfort searching for inner peace. Everybody with their faces enlightened by happiness. I can only summarize such a sacred experience by saying God exists. And that he expects to give us what he has brought us: His love which liberates and breaks the chains of slavery to the senses. A love that sits and installs us in the most comfortable of all thrones: his heart.

When you have finished reading this book, pay attention to what happens inside of you. You may feel a magical sensation; a kind of tickle in your heart. You won't be the same person who started to browse this book, perhaps misgiving, in the first pages. You have read a story as wonderful as it is real. That of a small being, dark-skinned, abundant hair, who was born and raised in a little rural town in southern India. The story of someone who has come here when society is submerged in chaos, having lost their love for God, forgetting basic moral principles. Someone who asks nothing in return for giving us everything. Who teaches by example. It's Bhagavan **Sri Sathya Sai Baba:** God as man, so that man may be God again.

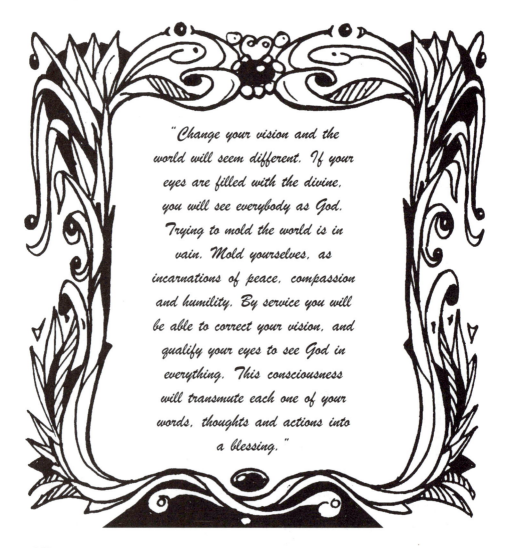

"Change your vision and the world will seem different. If your eyes are filled with the divine, you will see everybody as God. Trying to mold the world is in vain. Mold yourselves, as incarnations of peace, compassion and humility. By service you will be able to correct your vision, and qualify your eyes to see God in everything. This consciousness will transmute each one of your words, thoughts and actions into a blessing."

"All is God"

Glossary

Advaita: Highest philosophy in India. Basically it says All is God, there is nothing that is not. The objective is to become aware of God's immanence over Creation. It is opposed to the Duaita philosophy, in which it is said that creation is separated from God. In the first, God and man are One. In the second, man has to look for God somewhere other than himself. The Advaita is the vision Sai Baba teaches.

Ahimsa: Nonviolence.

Amritha: Nectar of the gods, ambrosial liquid Sai Baba materializes at times.

Ananda: Beatitude, joy. Beatitude is considered the very substance of God.

Arathi: Worshipping God with the camphor flame. It symbolizes the burning of the ego.

Arjuna: Hero of the Bhagavad Gita, in which he is guided by the avatar Krishna. It is the spiritual disciple's prototype.

Ashanti: Sorrow, anxiety (absence of peace).

Ashram: Establishment around a wise man or saint where spiritual and/or ascetic practices are done.

Atma: The Soul. The most subtle aspect of one's being; that which is immutable, unmodified, unaffected, eternal.

Avatar: Complete incarnation of God. Meaning it is born with a totally expanded consciousness.

Baba: Father.

Bahjans: Devotional songs.

Bal Vikas: Children educated in Sai Baba's teachings.

Bhagavad Gita: The Hindu Bible. It means The Song of God. It's part of the Mahabharata, India's great epic poem. It contains the teachings given by Lord Krishna to Arjuna and through him, to all mankind.

Bhagavad: Lord.

Bhagavan: Honorific title applied to fully realized saints.

Brahmins or Brahmans: Hinduist priests, members of the highest class among the Hindus, which does not imply a high economic position.

Brahma: Creative manifestation of God. God "the Creator" in the Hindu Trimurti; the other two are Vishnu and Shiva.

Brindavan: One of Sai Baba's universities.

Chakras: energy centers in the human body.

Chitravati: River of Puttaparthi where Sai Baba played in his childhood.

Darshan: Vision of the Divine. To enjoy the grace in the presence of a wise man. To see a holy person and receive his blessing.

Dharma: Rectitude, duty, code of conduct. One of the four ends humanity tries to achieve.

Ganges: Sacred river of India.

Guru: Spiritual master. He who moves the darkness away.

Japa: Recitative or repetition of the Lord's name.

Japamala: Religious collar of 108 beads. Rosary.

Jñana: The most elevated wisdom.

Karma: Action, law of cause and effect. Everything that happens is a result of a previous action. The action generates a cause and this cause in turn generates a consequence located in any time space.

Kumkum: Vermilion-colored powder put on the forehead.

Lila: The Lord's divine game. All Creation is His Lila.

Lingam: Ellipsoid shaped stone venerated as the symbol of the Creation.

Mahatma: Big soul.

Mandir: Temple.

Mantra: Sonic structure of power. Sacred formula whose sounds contain a great amount of energy. Its repetition grants equilibrium and peace of mind.

Maya: Ignorance which darkens the vision of God. Captivating primary illusion which appears as the duality called world. Attachment.

Nagar Sankirtan: Chants in group walking along the streets.

Om: Symbol of God. Primordial sound of the Creation. Its sound is divided into A U M. The A is located in the navel, representing the manifested, the body. The U is in the throat, representing the subtle. And the M is placed on the head, representing the causal. After pronouncing OM or AUM it is best to be quiet: it is in this silence that true contact with the Divinity is established.

Omkar: Reciting the OM 21 times.

Padnamaskar: Touch the feet in reverence.

Pandit: Erudite.

Paramatma: The Soul seen in its universal aspect of God.

Patanjali: Name of the ancient wise man who wrote the basic guide to Yoga.

Prana: Vital breath that supports life in the physical body and the Universe.

Prasad: Holy food.

Prashanti Nilayam: Name of Sai Baba's ashram. It means House of the Supreme Peace, in Puttaparthi.

Prema: The most intense and unconditional kind of divine love.

Purana: Book of Hindu mythology.

Rama: Avatar of God, divine being.

Ramakrishna (1836-1886): Great saint of Bengal.

Ramayana: Famous Hindu epic about the life of avatar Rama.

Sadhana: Spiritual discipline or practice.

Sadhu: Holy man, generally used to refer to a monk.

Samadhi: The perfect equanimity, void of highs and lows, untouched by joy or sorrow, communion with God.

Samsara: Sensory world which captivates the mind and gives way to insatiable desire, greed and suffering.

Samskaras: Tendencies inherent to a previous or past birth.

Sanathana Dharma: Ancient wisdom, eternal way of the truth.

Sanyasi: Person who has resigned to all and is completely immersed in God and the discipline to reach him.

Sarva Dharma: Emblem symbolizing the union of all religions.

Sathya: Sanskrit word meaning truth.

Seva: Sanskrit word meaning service.

Shatki: Divine creative power. Feminine aspect of God.

Shankaracharya: Hindu saint and philosopher.

Shirdi Sai Baba: Indian saint whose incarnation Sai Baba of Puttaparthi says he is.

Shiva: Third aspect of the Hindu triad. It represents the divinity's destructive character, destroying evil, to rebuild, regenerate and create again.

Siddhi: Personal perfection that includes the acquisition of superhuman powers.

Sri: Honorary title of respect meaning prosperity, abundance, majesty, dignity, luminosity. It precedes the name, used like Sir or Don.

Suprabatham: First dawn,morning prayer. Hymn or song which Sai Baba wakes up to every morning.

Swami: Honorary title meaning spiritual preceptor. Someone who has resigned to the world.

Telegu: Sai Baba's native language. Language of Andra Pradesh.

Upanishads: Mystic doctrines of Hinduism.

Vedanta: One of Hindu philosophy's six systems.

Vedas: Sanskrit word meaning revealed knowledge. Ancient teachings of Hinduism.

Vibhuti: Sacred ashes materialized by Sai Baba.

Vishnu: Manifestation of God "the preserver" in the Hindu Trimurti.

Whitefield: City thirteen miles from Bangalore, where Brindavan University of Sai Baba is located.

The Authors

Marcelo Berenstein is a writer and journalist. He was editor of *Construir* magazine and *Renacer* newspaper. He conducted radio programs and produces TV shows. He has known Sai Baba since 1985. He presided over the **Organización Sai Baba** of Argentina.

Miguel Angel Scenna, illustrator and comic strip artist, born in Bolívar, province of Buenos Aires, has collaborated for various written (*Clarín* newspaper, *First* magazine, *Renacer* newspaper) and editorial (*Columba, Record*) media. He also designed **Che Guevara for Beginners**.

Gratitude

To my father Sai, for creating me just the way I am. To my mother Sai, for lovingly showing me my faults and teaching me how to correct them. To my brother Sai, for making every instant of my life a game. To my friend Sai, for being my most loyal confident. To Gracielita, for loving and tolerating a husband who comes home and sits down to write isolating himself from the world. To my sons Iair and Joel, for reconnecting me with the world when isolation was already too much. To Dani Coifman, for his contributions and corrections. To Juan Carlos Kreimer, for confiding in me. To Carlitos Rivas, for being. —**Marcelo Berenstein.**

To Ricardo Parada, for his tips and editorial support —J.C.K.

ow to get original thinkers to come o your home...

ADDICTION & RECOVERY (£7.99)	HISTORY OF CLOWNS (£7.99)
ADLER (£7.99)	I CHING (£7.99)
AFRICAN HISTORY (£7.99)	JAZZ (£7.99)
ARABS & ISRAEL (£7.99)	JEWISH HOLOCAUST (£7.99)
ARCHITECTURE (£7.99)	JUDAISM (£7.99)
BABIES (£7.99)	JUNG (£7.99)
BENJAMIN (£7.99)	KIERKEGAARD (£7.99)
BIOLOGY (£7.99)	KRISHNAMURTI (£7.99)
BLACK HISTORY (£7.99)	LACAN (£7.99)
BLACK HOLOCAUST (£7.99)	MALCOLM X (£7.99)
BLACK PANTHERS (£7.99)	MAO (£7.99)
BLACK WOMEN (£7.99)	MARILYN (£7.99)
BODY (£7.99)	MARTIAL ARTS (£7.99)
BRECHT (£7.99)	MCLUHAN (£7.99)
BUDDHA (£7.99)	MILES DAVIS (£7.99)
CASATNEDA (£7.99)	NIETZSCHE (£7.99)
CHE (£7.99)	OPERA (£7.99)
CHOMSKY (£7.99)	PAN-AFRICANISM (£7.99)
CLASSICAL MUSIC (£7.99)	PHILOSOPHY (£7.99)
COMPUTERS (£7.99)	PLATO (£7.99)
THE HISTORY OF CINEMA (£9.99)	POSTMODERNISM (£7.99)
DERRIDA (£7.99)	STRUCTURALISM&
DNA (£7.99)	POSTSTRUCTURALISM (£7.99)
DOMESTIC VIOLENCE (£7.99)	PSYCHIATRY (£7.99)
THE HISTORY OF EASTERN EUROPE (£7.99)	RAINFORESTS (£7.99)
ELVIS (£7.99)	SAI BABA (£7.99)
ENGLISH LANGUAGE (£7.99)	SARTRE (£7.99)
EROTICA (£7.99)	SAUSSURE (£7.99)
FANON (£7.99)	SCOTLAND (£7.99)
FOOD (£7.99)	SEX (£7.99)
FOUCAULT (£7.99)	SHAKESPEARE (£7.99)
FREUD (£7.99)	STANISLAVSKI (£7.99)
GESTALT (£7.99)	UNICEF (£7.99)
HEALTH CARE (£7.99)	UNITED NATIONS (£7.99)
HEIDEGGER (£7.99)	US CONSTITUTION (£7.99)
HEMINGWAY (£7.99)	WORLD WAR II (£7.99)
ISLAM (£7.99)	ZEN (£7.99)

Individual Order Form   (clip out or copy complete page)

Book title	Quantity	Amount
	SUB TOTAL:	

U.S. only   N.Y. RESIDENTS ADD 8 1/4 SALES TAX:

Shipping & Handling ($3.00 for the first book; £.60 for each additional book):

	TOTAL	

BENJAMIN FOR BEGINNERS ™
Written and illustrated by
Lloyd Spencer
ISBN 0-86316-262-2
(U.K. £7.99)

Benjamin For Beginners ™
offers a clear accessible guide to
one of the most intriguing and
inspiring thinkers of the 20th
century. Since his suicide in
1940, the ideas of Walter
Benjamin have influenced
contemporary writers like
Jacques Derrida, Paul de Man,
George Steiner, John Berger and
Terry Eagleton. Today,
Benjamin's essays are hotly
debated by students of cultural
and media studies, by
philosophers and by literary
critics.

Benjamin wrote brilliant commenta
on major figures of literary moderni
including Baudelaire, Proust, Kafka
Brecht and the Surrealists. He wrote
a modernist and his preoccupation
questions of language and with liter
and artistic form extended to his
experimental ways of conceiving an
presenting his own writings.
Benjamin's writing is fragmentary,
highly idiosyncratic, some of it even
obscure. His major work, **The Paris**
Arcades, was left incomplete. He ai
to restore a 'heightened graphicness'
the understanding of history, drawir
on the emblem books of the 17th
century and on the example of
photomontage, as pioneered in his
day.

Benjamin For Beginners ™ uses the
possibilities offered by the format of
documentary comic book to further
extend Benjamin's experiments. It is
book which allows us to visualise w
is involved in Benjamin's most subth
and unfinished meditations, as well
in his most revolutionary and radica
gestures.

s new ?

In the summer of 1960, Carlos Castaneda was a student of Latin-American Anthropology, based in California. Academic logical reasoning had become ingrained in him. He was carrying out research into hallucinogenic plants in the Mexican desert. He met with the sorcerer Don Juan Matus, whose knowledge of the Toltec tradition went back thousands of years. Don Juan initiated Castaneda through a lengthy apprenticeship, which was by no means easy. During that time he saw all his convictions falling away, transforming himself despite himself, by entering into the magical universe pointed out to him by the sorcerer. Following the teachings passed on to him by Don Juan, Castaneda wrote a string of books describing his initiation, the other worlds discovered through new ways of seeing, and his experiences with the group of apprentices and sorcerers.

TENADA FOR BEGINNERS ™
Martin Broussalis
ustrated by Martin Arvallo
ISBN 0-86316-068-9
(U.K. £7.99)

In **Castaneda For Beginners**™, the Argentinean novelist Martin Broussalis follows the path of Castaneda through these new dimensions of knowledge, arriving at the present time and Castaneda's position of shaman, transmitting under the name of Tensegrity his range of energising exercises.

- Truth is a pathless land, you cannot approach it by any path whatsoever, by any religion, by any sect. Truth, being limitless, unconditioned, unapproachable by any path whatsoever, cannot be organized; nor any organization be formed to lead or coerce people along any particular path -   -J. Krishnamurti

Jiddu Krishnamurti was one of the great thinkers of this time. Until his death in 1986 at the age of ninety, Krishnamurti travelled the world speaking and teaching people to free themselves of their *own* mental bondage and endeavour to gain

harmony with themselves. He taught that mankind has created the environment in which he lives and that nothing can ever put a stop to violence and suffering except a transformation in the human psyche.

Krishnamurti For Beginners ™ explores the theories of the great philosopher and gives the reader a look at how his ideas have shaped educational philosophy and philosophy in general. In witty text and illustration the book explains key principles of Krishnamurt's doctrine detailing his legacy of non violence and his continued resistance against dogmatic thinking of all kinds.

SHNAMURTI FOR BEGINNERS ™
Juan Carlos Kreimer
ustrated by Martin Arvallo
ISBN 0- 86316-068-9
(U.K. £7.99)

accept no substitute

Great ideas and great thinkers can be
thrilling. They can also be intimidating

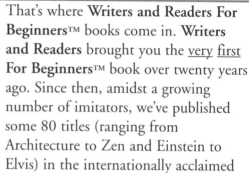

That's where **Writers and Readers For Beginners**™ books come in. **Writers and Readers** brought you the <u>very</u> <u>first</u> **For Beginners**™ book over twenty years ago. Since then, amidst a growing number of imitators, we've published some 80 titles (ranging from Architecture to Zen and Einstein to Elvis) in the internationally acclaimed **For Beginners**™ series. Every book in the series serves one purpose: to UNintimidate and UNcomplicate the works of the great thinkers. Knowledge is too important to be confined to the experts.

And Knowledge as you will discover in our **Documentary Comic Books,** is fun! Each book is painstakingly researched, humorously written and illustrated in whatever style best suits the subject at hand. That's where **Writers and Readers, For Beginners**™ books began! Remember if it doesn't say...

Writers and Readers

...it's not an original For Beginners book.